3. **Place** a toothpick through each straw. (If necessary, you can tape toothpicks together to make them longer.)

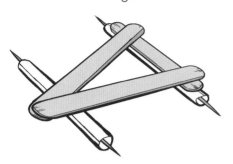

4. With an adult's help, **poke** a hole big enough to insert the toothpicks into the bottle caps.

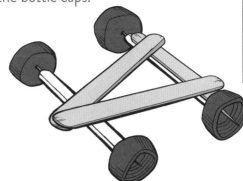

Test your racer. Can it roll for 10 seconds? 20 seconds? For how many groups of 10 seconds can you get it to roll?

LET'S ENGINEER!

D1232591

Last year, Enid raced in the MotMot Grand Prix and came in second place. This year, she's determined to win.

How can Enid modify her racer so she can go faster and come in first place?

Set a starting line and a finish line. **Get** your racer from the Let's Make activity and time how long it takes to get from start to finish before making any changes to the racer. Now **look** at your materials and think about how you built your racer—what changes might make a faster racer?

Modify your racer to make it go faster. **Time** your racer again. Was it faster? Slower? If so, why?

PROJECT 1: DONE!
Get your sticker!

Skip Counting to 1,000

Skip the stones by following the instructions below.

Callie wants to skip her stone by **fives**. Draw how her stone bounces.

Dimitri wants to skip his stone by **tens**. Draw how his stone bounces.

Enid wants to skip her stone by **hundreds**. Draw how her stone bounces.

Frank has a remote control stone that skips forever. Count by fives and fill in the missing numbers where the stone bounces.

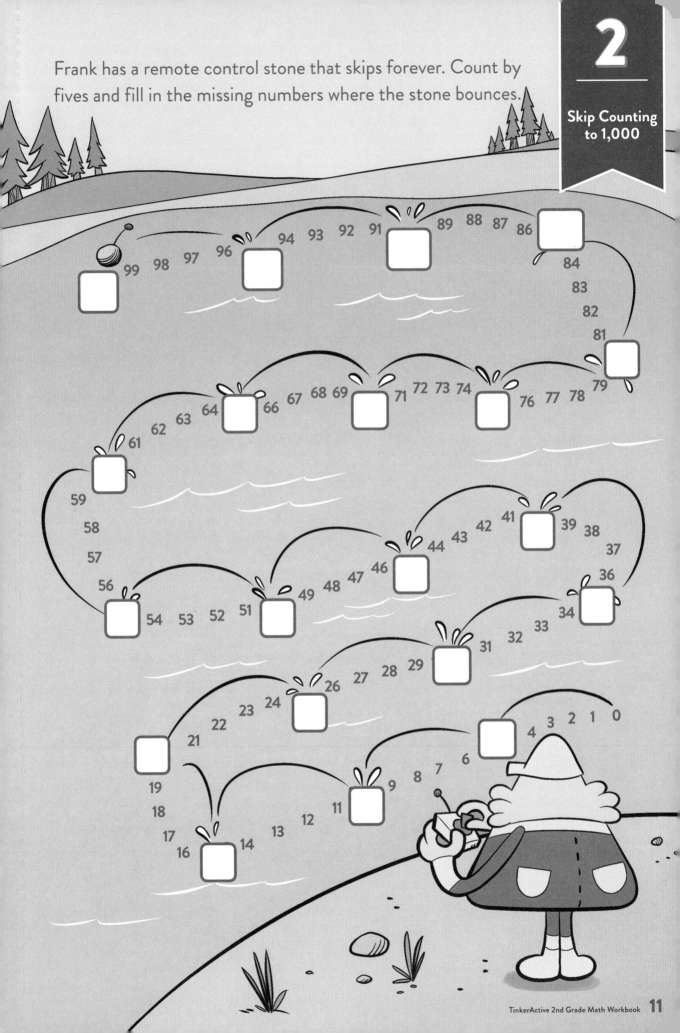

99 98 97 96 94 93 92 91 [ ] 89 88 87 86 [ ]
84
83
82
81
[ ] 79 78 77 76 [ ] 74 73 72 71 [ ] 69 68 67 66 [ ] 64 63 62 61 [ ]
59
58
57
56 [ ] 54 53 52 51 [ ] 49 48 47 46 [ ] 44 43 42 41 [ ] 39 38
37
36
34 [ ]
33 32 31 [ ] 29 28 27 26 [ ] 24 23 22 21 [ ]
19
18
17 16 [ ] 14 13 12 11 [ ] 9 8 7 6 [ ] 4 3 2 1 0

Write the next number in the pattern. Read each answer aloud.

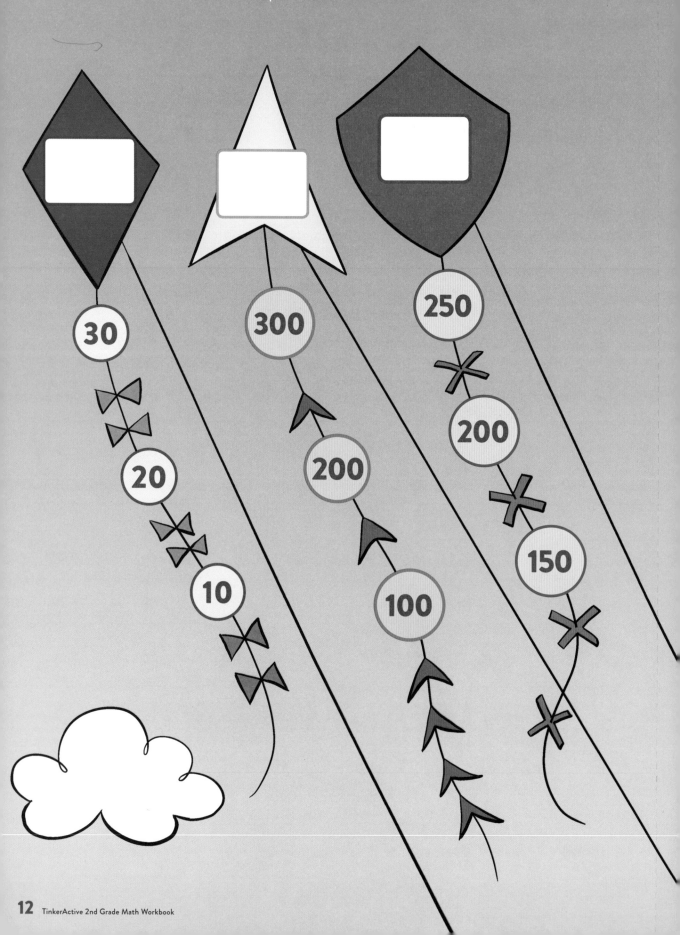

30

300

250

20

200

200

10

100

150

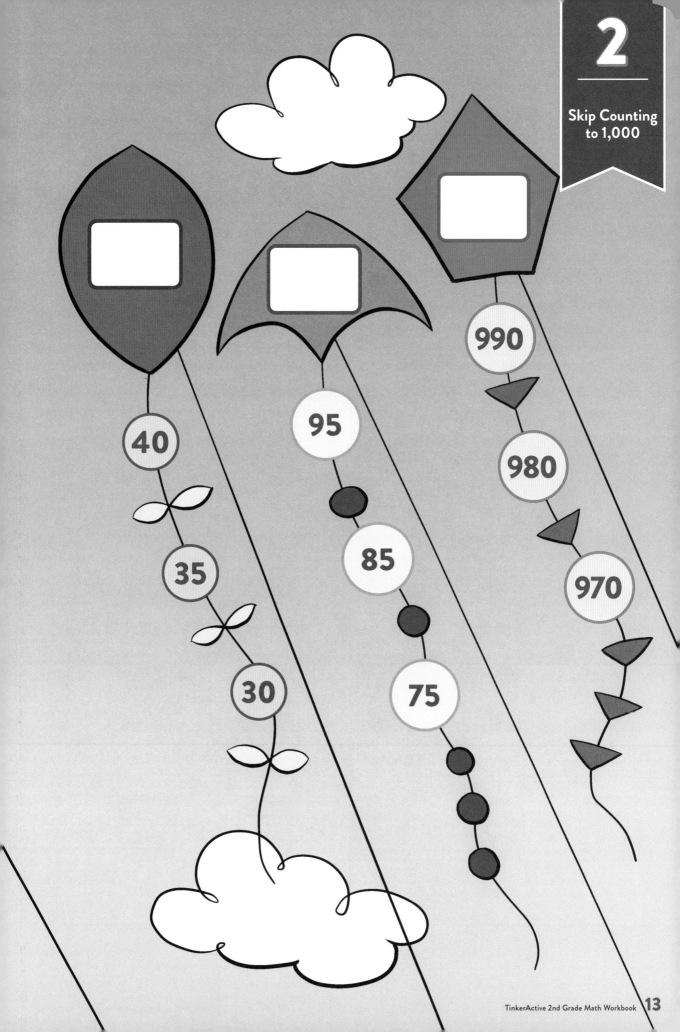

40

35

30

95

85

75

990

980

970

Starting at 905, count by fives aloud and draw a circle around each number you say.

Next, starting at 910, count by tens aloud and draw a square around each number you say.

Last, starting at 950, count by fifties aloud and draw a triangle around each number you say.

901	902	903	904	905	906	907	908	909	910
911	912	913	914	915	916	917	918	919	920
921	922	923	924	925	926	927	928	929	930
931	932	933	934	935	936	937	938	939	940
941	942	943	944	945	946	947	948	949	950
951	952	953	954	955	956	957	958	959	960
961	962	963	964	965	966	967	968	969	970
971	972	973	974	975	976	977	978	979	980
981	982	983	984	985	986	987	988	989	990
991	992	993	994	995	996	997	998	999	1,000

Put your fingers on 50, 100, and 150. Then count by fifties and move a finger to the next number. (Hint: Your next move is to put a finger on 200.) Try to keep two fingers on the page at all times and skip count to 1,000.

LET'S START! GATHER THESE TOOLS AND MATERIALS.

30 small stones

30 pennies

40 pieces of dried beans, pasta, cereal, or nuts

Rice

Permanent markers

3 empty plastic bottles

3 balloons

LET'S TINKER!

Sort the stones, pennies, dried beans, and rice grains into groups of 10.

Line up each group at the edge of a sink full of water and flick each object so it skips. Do all your materials skip? What if you position them differently? How many skips can you make with each type of object?

LET'S MAKE: MOTMOT RAFT!

1. **Ask** an adult to cut a plastic bottle into the shape below.

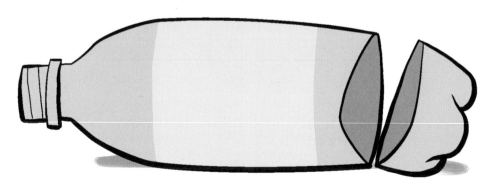

5 handfuls of semisweet chocolate chips

1 cup milk

2 cups plain yogurt

Measuring cup

Mixing bowl and spoon

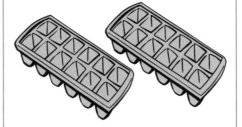

2 ice cube trays

40 craft sticks

LET'S TINKER!

Grab a handful of chocolate chips. **Count** how many you can hold. Is it an even or odd number?

Now **arrange** the chocolate chips in groups of two to check!

LET'S MAKE: ICE POPS!

1. With the help of an adult, **mix** 1 cup yogurt with $\frac{1}{2}$ cup milk.

2. Melt 2 handfuls of chocolate chips in the microwave.

3. Combine the melted chocolate into the yogurt-milk mixture.

4. Pour the mixture into an ice cube tray.

5. Poke craft sticks into each compartment. **Freeze** for at least 6 hours.

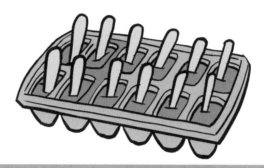

LET'S ENGINEER!

Frank likes chocolate ice pops. But he likes chocolate-chip chocolate ice pops even better. He has some leftover chocolate chips and wants to drop them into his pops evenly.

How can Frank make sure he puts the same amount of chocolate chips in each ice pop?

Follow the directions for ice pops again. Before you put the tray in the freezer, **drop** the same amount of leftover chocolate chips in each ice pop. Did you drop an even amount or an odd amount of chocolate chips into each one?

PROJECT 4: DONE!
Get your sticker!

Addition & Subtraction

You can solve a subtraction problem by thinking of the related addition problem.

Solve each set of problems.

$$\begin{array}{r} 7 \\ -\ 3 \\ \hline \square \end{array}$$

$$\begin{array}{r} 3 \\ +\ \square \\ \hline 7 \end{array}$$

$$\begin{array}{r} 14 \\ -\ 6 \\ \hline \square \end{array}$$

$$\begin{array}{r} 6 \\ +\ \square \\ \hline 14 \end{array}$$

$$\begin{array}{r} 15 \\ -\ 9 \\ \hline \square \end{array}$$

$$\begin{array}{r} 9 \\ +\ \square \\ \hline 15 \end{array}$$

Use the treehouse chart below to solve the problems on the next page. Put your finger on the first number and then add or subtract by moving your finger by tens and then by ones. Fill in the sentences and write your answer.

1	2	3	4	5	6	7	8	9	10
11	12	13	14	15	16	17	18	19	20
21	22	23	24	25	26	27	28	29	30
31	32	33	34	35	36	37	38	39	40
41	42	43	44	45	46	47	48	49	50
51	52	53	54	55	56	57	58	59	60
61	62	63	64	65	66	67	68	69	70
71	72	73	74	75	76	77	78	79	80
81	82	83	84	85	86	87	88	89	90
91	92	93	94	95	96	97	98	99	100

43 + 17 = 60

- Start at 43.
- Jump __10__ spaces forward.
- Then move __7__ more spaces forward.

74 – 19 = ☐

- Start at 74.
- Jump _____ spaces backward.
- Then move _____ more spaces backward.

25 + 28 = ☐

- Start at 25.
- Jump _____ spaces forward.
- Then move _____ more spaces forward.

93 – 19 = ☐

- Start at 93.
- Jump _____ spaces backward.
- Then move _____ more spaces backward.

18 + 53 = ☐

- Start at 18.
- Jump _____ spaces forward.
- Then move _____ more spaces forward.

55 – 26 = ☐

- Start at 55.
- Jump _____ spaces backward.
- Then move _____ more spaces backward.

46 + 16 = ☐

- Start at 46.
- Jump _____ spaces forward.
- Then move _____ more spaces forward.

84 – 77 = ☐

- Start at 84.
- Jump _____ spaces backward.
- Then move _____ more spaces backward.

Cut out the rooms in the tree house. Arrange each in the grid so every row and column adds up to 15.

1	2	3
4	5	6
7	8	9

5	1	9	15
3	8	4	15
7	6	2	15
15	15	15	

2			15
			15
	3	8	15
15	15	15	

7			15
			15
3	4		15
15	15	15	

Arrange the rooms so each row or column adds up to the number outside the grid.

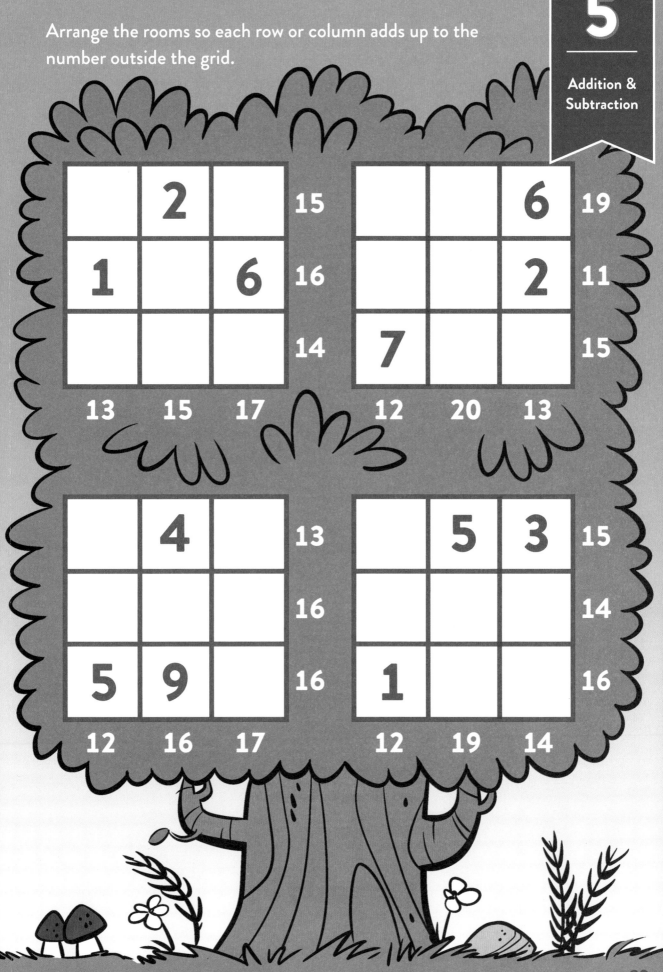

Grid 1:

	2		15
1		6	16
			14
13	15	17	

Grid 2:

		6	19
		2	11
7			15
12	20	13	

Grid 3:

	4		13
			16
5	9		16
12	16	17	

Grid 4:

	5	3	15
			14
1			16
12	19	14	

LET'S START! GATHER THESE TOOLS AND MATERIALS.

1 small cup

40 coins

30 or more craft sticks

20 straws

Paper

10 clothespins or binder clips

Masking tape

Glue

LET'S TINKER!

Place the cup on a table. **Toss** your coins one by one into the cup from a few feet away until you are out of coins. How many coins did you get into the cup? **Count** the number of coins that landed in the cup. Now, without counting, **determine** how many coins missed the cup.

LET'S MAKE: TREE HOUSE!

1. Lay 10–12 craft sticks in a row.

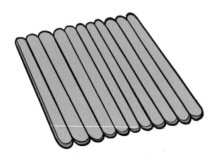

2. Glue 3 sticks across to make the platform of your tree house.

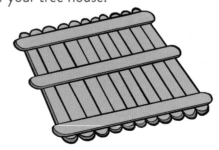

3. Using the rest of your craft sticks, **build** walls.

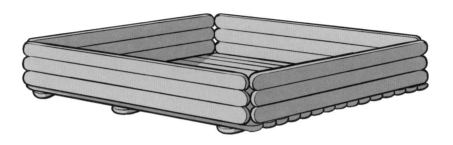

How many craft sticks did you use for each part of the tree house? **Add** the craft sticks used for the floor and walls together. How many did you use in all?

LET'S ENGINEER!

Enid wants to build a table to put in her tree house. She wants to make sure it can hold a bucket of cookies for her and all her friends.

How can Enid build a table that will hold all her cookies?

Using your materials, **build** a table that can support a cup of coins. Put your cup on top and start adding coins. How many coins can it hold up before breaking?

PROJECT 5: DONE!
Get your sticker!

Addition Using Place Value

Look at each addition sentence. Then look at each number as an array. Circle any groups of 10 blocks in the ones place, and circle any groups of 10 blocks in the tens place. Then solve.

21 + 14 = _35_

	Tens	Ones
21	■ ■	■
+ 14	■	■ ■ ■ ■

37 + 22 = ____

	Tens	Ones
37	■ ■ ■	■ ■ ■ ■ ■ ■ ■
+ 22	■ ■	■ ■

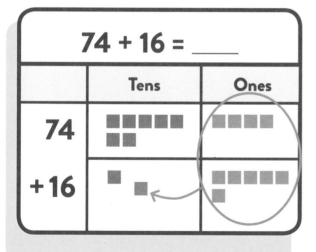

74 + 16 = ____

	Tens	Ones
74	■ ■ ■ ■ ■ ■ ■	■ ■ ■ ■
+ 16	■ ■	■ ■ ■ ■ ■ ■

32 + 18 = ____

	Tens	Ones
32	■ ■ ■	■ ■
+ 18	■	■ ■ ■ ■ ■ ■ ■ ■

86 + 25 + 18 = _____

	Hundreds	Tens	Ones
86		■■■■■ ■■■	■■■■■ ■
25		■■	■■■■■
+18		■	■■■■■ ■■■

63 + 58 + 12 = _____

	Hundreds	Tens	Ones
63		■■■■■ ■	■■■
58		■■■■■	■■■■■ ■■■
+12		■	■■

Look at each addition sentence. Then color the blocks in the tens columns and ones columns for each number. Then add.

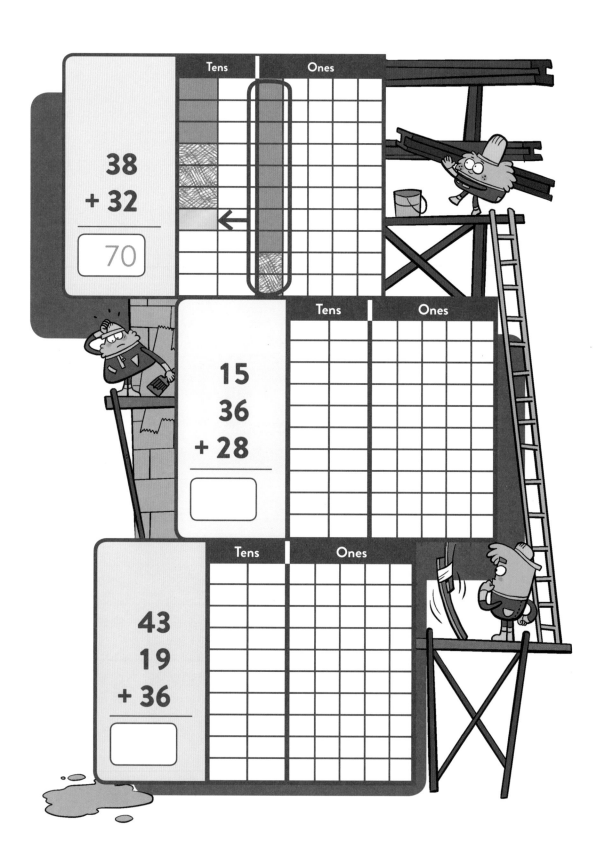

38
+ 32
70

15
36
+ 28

43
19
+ 36

	Tens	Ones
27		
48		
+ 16		

	Tens	Ones
13		
29		
+ 47		

	Tens	Ones
48		
36		
+ 15		

Draw blocks in the place value chart to represent each number in the number sentence. Then add. Circle and carry bundles of tens or hundreds when necessary.

	Hundreds	Tens	Ones
65 + 75 **140**			

	Hundreds	Tens	Ones
74 + 16			

	Hundreds	Tens	Ones
86 25 + 18			

	Hundreds	Tens	Ones
68 38 + 13			

Use place value to solve each problem. Wherever possible, make 10 ones or 10 tens to simplify the problem.

25 + **15** = 40

20 + 5 + 10 + 5

30 + 10 = 40

28 + **12** + **36** = _____

20 + 8 + 10 + 2 + 30 + 6

59 + **51** + **33** = _____

19 + **41** + **23** = _____

LET'S START!

GATHER THESE TOOLS AND MATERIALS.

4 dice

Paper

Markers

Scissors
(with an adult's help)

10 or more beans

10 or more pieces of dried pasta

10 or more cotton balls

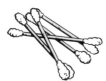
10 or more cotton swabs

Tape or glue

LET'S TINKER!

Separate the four dice into groups of two. **Roll** each set of dice and record the numbers on a piece of paper. For example, if you roll a **1** and a **6** with one pair of dice, record the number as **16** or **61**—it's your choice. Then roll the other pair of dice for your second number. **Add** the two numbers together. What is the sum? Can you add the numbers in your head?

LET'S MAKE: SPINNER GAME!

1. Draw 2 large circles on 2 pieces of paper and cut them out.

2. Draw lines to divide each circle into 6 equal wedges and write a 2-digit number between 20 and 50 in each wedge.

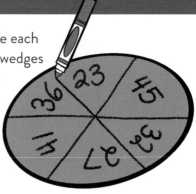

3. Place a marker in the middle of one circle as the spinner.

4. Play: Spin the marker and, on a separate piece of paper, record the number the cap of the marker lands on. **Repeat** with the other circle. **Add** the numbers together to get a sum. Now it's the other player's turn to do the same. Whoever is closest to 100 wins the round. Keep playing until one player wins three rounds.

LET'S ENGINEER!

The MotMots are competing in a crafting contest! They have to use 10 or more dried beans, 10 or more pieces of pasta, 10 or more cotton balls, and 10 or more cotton swabs to create a sculpture that looks like their favorite animal.

How can the MotMots design an animal sculpture using all those materials?

Construct your sculpture using 10 or more of each item listed. Make sure you **record** how many of each item you are using. **Add** up the number of items you used to make your sculpture. What is the sum? Can you make a sculpture using more materials? How many more items did you add?

PROJECT 6: DONE!
Get your sticker!

Draw the rest of each rope by connecting the expanded form of each number.

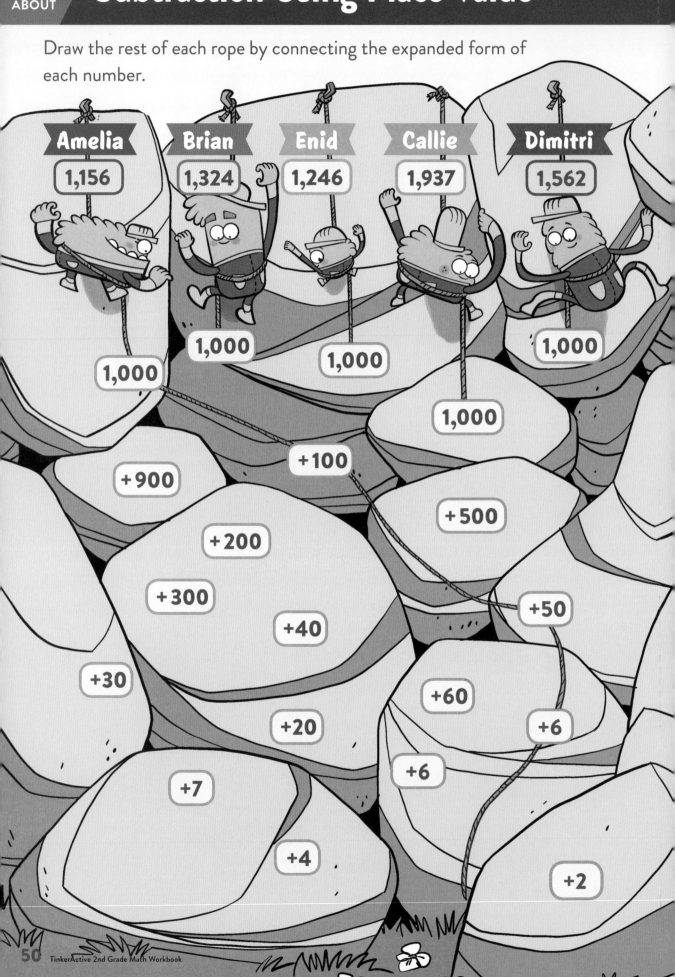

Subtract by using place value.

7

Subtraction Using Place Value

70 − 40 = ☐

7 tens − 4 tens =

____

53 − 20 = ☐

5 tens, 3 ones − 2 tens =

____

77 − 60 = ☐

7 tens, 7 ones − 6 tens =

____

59 − 28 = ☐

5 tens, 9 ones − 2 tens, 8 ones =

____

45 − 33 = ☐

4 tens, 5 ones − 3 tens, 3 ones =

____

Subtract by using the expanded number form and jumping hundreds, tens, and ones.

34 − 11 = 23

−10   −1
34 → 24 → 23

48 − 35 =

−30   −5
48 → 18 → ___

68 − 17 =

86 − 48 =

643 − 126 = [ ]

427 − 213 = [ ]

866 − 542 = [ ]

981 − 580 = [ ]

Use the place value chart to solve each problem.

	Tens	Ones
39 – 12 = 27	● ● ⊗	● ● ● ● ● ● ● ⊗ ⊗
	2	7

	Tens	Ones
58 – 26 =		

	Tens	Ones
76 – 43 =		

	Tens	Ones
98 – 25 =		

The MotMots are packing their backpacks for a nature hike!
Draw a place value chart to solve each word problem.

Enid decided to pack **183** of her favorite cotton balls. But then she decided she didn't need **72** of them, so she unpacked them. How many does she have packed?

Frank packed **175** egg sandwiches, but he ate **30** of them. How many does he have left?

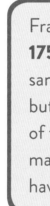

Dimitri packed **432** rubber bands. Callie packed **100** fewer. How many did Callie pack?

LET'S START!

GATHER THESE TOOLS AND MATERIALS.

Bowl of popcorn

Brushes

Paint, including:
black; **red**, **pink**, or **orange**; **yellow** or **green**;
blue or **purple**

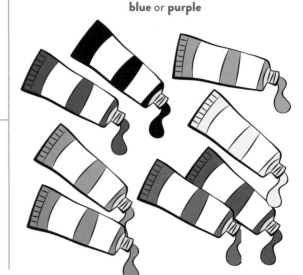

30 flat stones
(10 large, 10 medium, 10 small)

LET'S TINKER!

Get a bowl of popcorn. **Count** each kernel in the bowl. **Eat** five! How many kernels do you have left? **Keep** eating, taking handfuls of 5, 10, 50, and 100 (you can use two hands!) at a time, and subtracting from the total.

LET'S MAKE: STACKING STONES!

1. Find 10 large stones, 10 medium stones, and 10 small stones. They should be large and flat enough for stacking. **Wash** and dry each stone.

2. Paint the large stones red, pink, or orange. **Let** them dry and write "100" on them with black paint.

3. Paint the medium stones yellow or green. **Let** them dry and write "10" on them with black paint.

4. Paint the small stones blue or purple. **Let** them dry and write "1" on them with black paint.

What numbers can you make by stacking stones together? For example, if you stack a red 100 stone, a yellow 10 stone, and a purple 1 stone, what number do you make? (111!) What happens to that number when you remove one of the stones?

LET'S ENGINEER!

The MotMots are creating their own numbers with their stacking stones. Enid's stack has a value of 434. Brian's stack has a value of 376. Callie wants to build a stack that is exactly the value of Enid's stack minus the value of Brian's stack.

How can Callie find out the value of her stack without writing it down?

Figure out the value of Callie's stack using only the stones, and then build it.

PROJECT 7: DONE!
Get your sticker!

Addition & Subtraction: Word Problems

Solve the word problems below.

At the Cotton Ball Festival, Amelia ate 9 pies. Then she ate 4 more. Enid ate 2 pies. How many pies did they eat altogether?

Brian won 19 tickets, and Amelia won 24 more tickets than Brian. How many tickets did Amelia win?

Brian got to level 5 in the strength contest. He tried again and reached 3 levels higher. On his third try, he reached 4 levels higher than on his second try. How high did he get?

Frank's cotton ball won the Fluff and Stuff competition by beating 27 other contestants. In the Bounce and Flounce competition, he beat 10 other contestants. And in the Wiggle and Waggle competition, he beat 2 others. How many contestants did he beat in total?

Enid won 27 prizes, and Amelia won 5 fewer prizes than Enid. How many prizes did Amelia win?

Callie stayed on the Spin Cycle ride for 12 seconds. The next time, she rode for a shorter amount of time. In total, she rode for 20 seconds. How long was her second ride?

Read the story. As you read, tally the costume photos on page 61 by drawing circles (O) to add or crossing circles out (Ø) to subtract.

Dimitri ran around the Cotton Ball Festival to take photos of all the different costumes. He saw **10** cowboy cotton balls in the cafeteria and **2** more by the water fountain.

He spotted **14** astronaut cotton balls on the trampolines. Then **4** more arrived. But then **10** of them took off their helmets and they were actually pirates!

Another **12** pirates were standing by the donut truck, along with **4** more cowboys.

Finally, in the dance hall at the Cotton Ball, he saw **7** cowboys, **2** pirates, **7** ninjas, and **1** astronaut.

That was when Dimitri saw that his camera's battery was almost dead. As he replaced the battery, he accidentally erased pictures of **10** cowboys and **3** astronauts.

Can you write your own word problem using cotton balls?

By the end of the night, how many pictures of each costume did he have?

cowboys: _____

ninjas: _____

astronauts: _____

pirates: _____

Fill in the number sentences to solve. Then draw a line from each MotMot to the prize they can get using all their tickets.

Dimitri won **73** tickets from the carnival games. He gave **20** away. Then he won another **17**.

Step 1: 73 – 20 = __53__

Step 2: __53__ + 17 = __70__

Frank won **84** tickets for his prize cotton ball. He won another **11** for the dance competition. Then he lost **20** through a hole in his pocket.

Step 1: 84 + 11 = ____

Step 2: ____ – 20 = ____

Callie won **81** tickets. She accidentally lost **30** of them when she went on the Spin Cycle ride. Then she won another **23**.

Step 1: 81 – 30 = ____

Step 2: _____

Enid won only **9** tickets because she could not see over the counter. Amelia gave her **65** tickets to make her feel better. But **40** of those tickets were covered in cherry pie and couldn't be used.

Step 1: _____

Step 2: _____

20 or more cotton balls

Construction paper

Scissors
(with an adult's help)

Glue

20 or more craft sticks

10 or more rubber bands

3 or more bottle caps

Bucket or basket

LET'S TINKER!

Decorate the cotton balls as cowboys, astronauts, pirates, and ninjas. **Cut** out 3 cowboy hats from your construction paper for 3 cowboys. **Cut** out 5 helmets for 5 astronauts. **Cut** out 4 eye patches for 4 pirates. **Cut** out 5 throwing stars for 5 ninjas.

Glue the items above to your cotton balls. How many cottons balls are dressed up in total?

LET'S MAKE: COTTON-BALL CATAPULT!

1. Stack 3 craft sticks together and wrap each end with a rubber band.

2. Do the same with another 2 craft sticks, but wrap only one end with a rubber band.

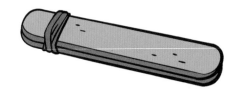

3. Place the stack of 3 craft sticks in between the stack of 2 craft sticks and attach them with a rubber band where they overlap.

4. Glue a bottle cap to the end of the top craft stick.

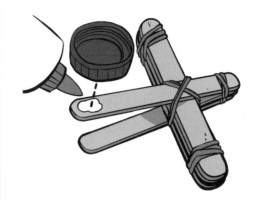

Your catapult is finished! **Shoot** a cotton ball with your catapult.

Modify your catapult by adding or subtracting craft sticks, rubber bands, and bottle caps. Does this change the accuracy of your catapult or how far your cotton ball can go?

LET'S ENGINEER!

The MotMots are playing a game of Toss That Cotton Ball! The MotMots get points for each cotton ball that goes into a bucket across the room. The pirates are worth 9 points. The astronauts are worth 7. The cowboys are worth 16. The ninjas are worth 24. Callie needs to get more than 47 points to beat Frank's record.

How can Callie beat Frank's record?

Use the catapult you made to launch the cotton balls into your bucket. **Try** to beat Frank's record for Callie. **Alter** the design of the catapult to make it shoot farther and be more accurate.

PROJECT 8: DONE!
Get your sticker!

Measurement

Every Thursday, the MotMots have a stacking competition. Measure each stack of MotMots in inches or in centimeters.

inches

centimeters

inches

inches

centimeters

centimeters

MotMots love to measure, so they have lots of measuring devices.
Circle the best tool to measure each object.

Ruler

Yardstick

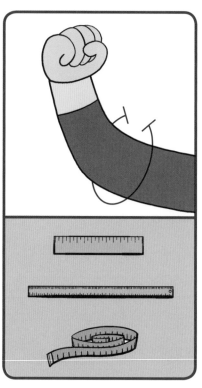
Measuring tape

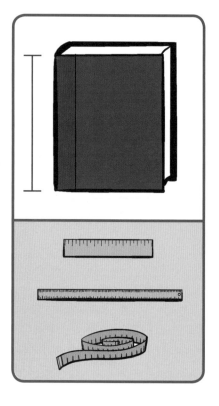

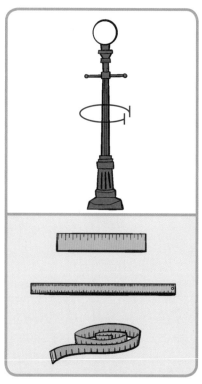

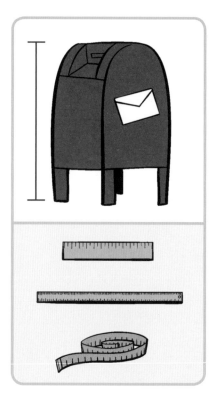

Circle the best unit of measurement for each object. Then estimate how tall each object is.

inches **feet yards**

Estimation: _____

inches **feet yards**

Estimation: _____

inches feet yards

Estimation: _____

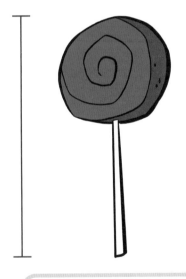

inches feet yards

Estimation: _____

Estimate the length of your own arm and then measure it. How close was the actual measurement to your guess?

Put your hand on the page and trace around it. Then use a ruler to measure each finger in inches and in centimeters. Write your measurements next to each finger. Then measure the length of your whole hand in inches and in centimeters and write your measurements below.

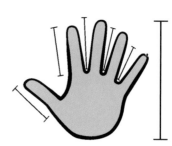

My hand is _____ inches or _____ centimeters long.

Put your foot on the page and trace around it. Then measure the length of your foot in inches and in centimeters. Write your measurements below.

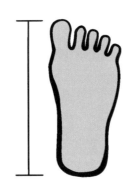

My foot is _____ inches or _____ centimeters long.

LET'S START! GATHER THESE TOOLS AND MATERIALS.

5 bottle caps

Tape measure

Scissors
(with an adult's help)

Rubber band

2 beads or pieces
of dried tube pasta

Tape

Ruler

Markers

LET'S TINKER!

Find a large, smooth surface, like a countertop or an uncarpeted floor.

Slide the bottle caps across the surface. **Try** flicking, hitting, or sliding the caps. Is it easier to slide some bottle caps than others? Do some caps go farther than others?

Estimate how far each bottle cap slid. Then **use** your tape measure to measure the distances.

LET'S MAKE: MOTMOT LAUNCHER!

1. Cut the rubber band.

2. Thread each end of the rubber band through a bead or a piece of pasta.

3. Knot the ends to create handles.

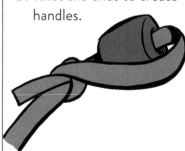

4. Get stickers from page 129 and decorate your bottle caps.

5. Launch the bottle caps by snapping your rubber band, and measure how far they fly.

LET'S ENGINEER!

Frank has been working on his Frank Launcher. It's finally able to launch Frank, but he can't control how far he goes. So if he tries it, he won't know where he'll land!

How can Frank modify his launcher so he goes exactly as far as he wants?

Stretch a tape measure on a table. **Stand** a marker up at a distance you think you can hit. Now **try** to knock it down by launching a bottle cap from your MotMot launcher. Did you knock over the marker? If not, **modify** the cap or launcher to try to hit it. If you did knock over the marker, **measure** another distance and try hitting that as well. How can you modify your cap or launcher to hit the marker at a different distance?

PROJECT 9: DONE!
Get your sticker!

Length

Estimate the length and height of each train. Then use a ruler to measure each train.

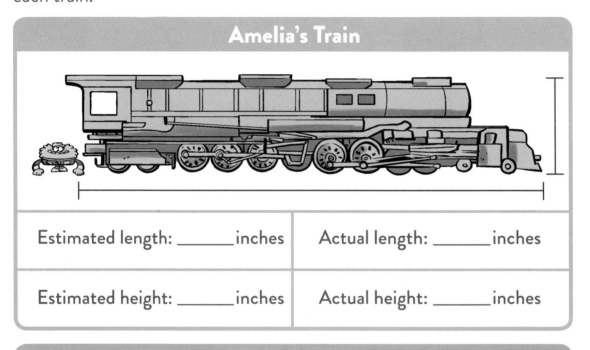

Amelia's Train

Estimated length: _____ inches | Actual length: _____ inches

Estimated height: _____ inches | Actual height: _____ inches

Brian's Train

Estimated length: _____ inches | Actual length: _____ inches

Estimated height: _____ inches | Actual height: _____ inches

Which train is longer? _____

How much longer is the longer train? _____

Which train is taller? _____

How much taller is the taller train? _____

Amelia's shovel is 6 inches longer than Brian's. Brian's shovel is 52 inches long. How long is Amelia's?

_____ inches

The crossing sign on Amelia's track is 10 centimeters shorter than Brian's. Brian's sign is 81 centimeters tall. How tall is Amelia's?

_____ centimeters

Amelia's steam whistle is 54 inches long. Brian's whistle is 14 inches shorter than Amelia's. How long is Brian's whistle?

_____ inches

Use the number lines to solve the following problems.

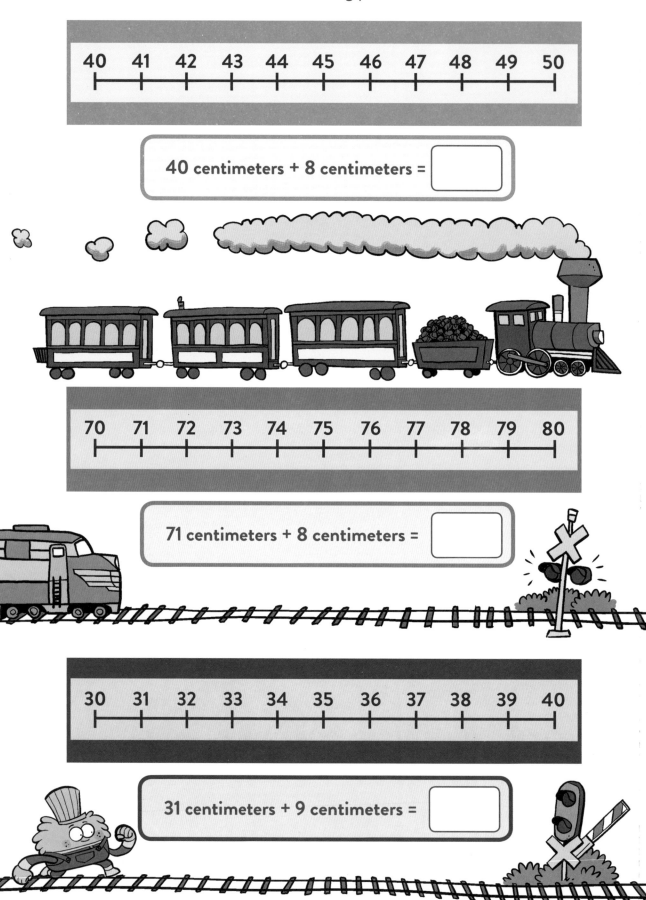

40 41 42 43 44 45 46 47 48 49 50

40 centimeters + 8 centimeters = [ ]

70 71 72 73 74 75 76 77 78 79 80

71 centimeters + 8 centimeters = [ ]

30 31 32 33 34 35 36 37 38 39 40

31 centimeters + 9 centimeters = [ ]

Draw number lines to solve the following problems.

31 centimeters + 16 centimeters = [ ]

56 centimeters + 9 centimeters = [ ]

65 centimeters + 12 centimeters = [ ]

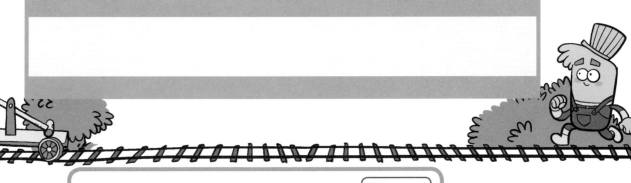

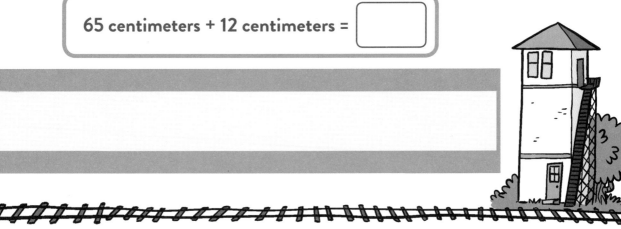

Get a few pencils and measure them. How long is the longest pencil? How long is the shortest pencil? How much longer is the longest pencil than the shortest?

Measure each track in inches.

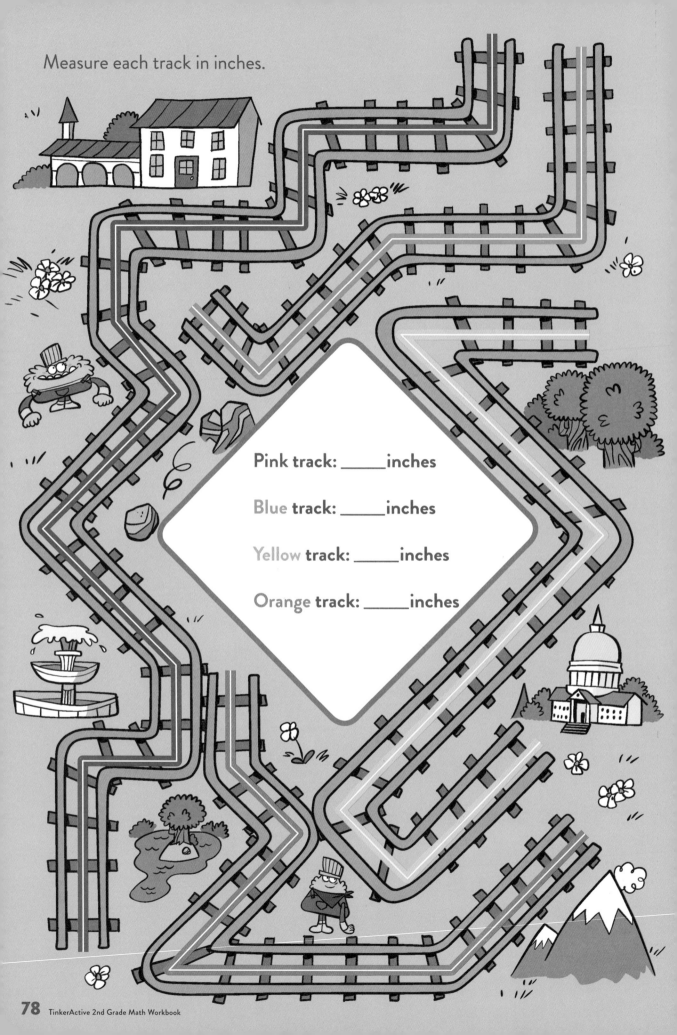

Pink track: _____ inches

Blue track: _____ inches

Yellow track: _____ inches

Orange track: _____ inches

Which path is shorter, **pink** or **blue**?

Which path is longer, **yellow** or **pink**?

How much shorter or longer is the **yellow** track than the **pink**?

If Amelia took the **pink** path, and Brian waited for her to get exactly halfway before starting on the **blue** path, who would have the shorter distance left to walk?

How much shorter or longer is the **orange** track than the **blue** ?

How much shorter or longer is the **yellow** track than the **orange**?

LET'S START! GATHER THESE TOOLS AND MATERIALS.

Cardboard

10–15 marbles

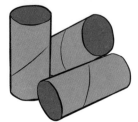
2 or more toilet paper or paper towel rolls

50 craft sticks

Tape

Scissors (with an adult's help)

Glue sticks or glue gun

LET'S TINKER!

Roll a marble on different surfaces, like tables, carpets, and tile.

Measure how far it rolls on each surface.

How much farther does the marble go on one surface versus another?

LET'S MAKE: MARBLE RUN!

1. **Glue** craft sticks together to make trays.

2. **Cut** toilet paper rolls to create more trays.

3. Glue or tape the trays to cardboard to create the run.

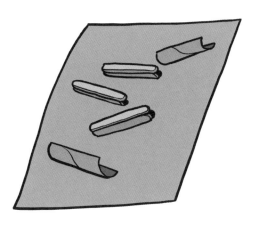

4. Tape the cardboard to a wall and test your marble run!

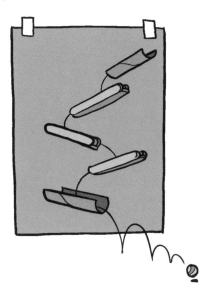

How long is your marble run? Measure each tray and add the lengths.

LET'S ENGINEER!

Enid is perfectly round, and that makes her perfectly suited for the MotMot Marble Madness Marathon. She wants to go at least 100 centimeters.

How can Enid roll more than 100 centimeters?

Extend your run so a marble can travel more than 100 centimeters. Remember, if a marble drops from one tray to another, you can count the distance between the trays.

PROJECT 10: DONE!
Get your sticker!

Time

Draw a line to match the time on the clocks.

Draw the hands on the clocks to show
when each MotMot finished the course.

CALLIE 12:00

DIMITRI 2:15

BRIAN 3:30

AMELIA 2:45

ENID 1:35

FRANK 2:20

Count by fives to tell the time. Then fill in the missing numbers in each sentence.

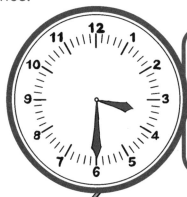

The clock shows _____ minutes after _____ o'clock.

It's _____ : _____ _____

The clock shows _____ minutes after _____ o'clock.

It's _____ : _____ _____

The clock shows _____ minutes after _____ o'clock.

It's _____ : _____ _____

The clock shows

_____ minutes after

_____ o'clock.

It's _____ : _____ _____

The clock shows

_____ minutes after

_____ o'clock.

It's _____ : _____ _____

When do you do each activity? Draw hands on the clock. Then fill in the missing time in the sentence, as well as a.m. or p.m.

I wake up at ___ : _____

I eat breakfast at ___ : _____

I go to school at ___ : _____

I eat lunch at ___ : _____

I have recess at ___ : _____

I go home at ___ : _____

I eat dinner at ___ : _____

I go to bed at ___ : _____

Cut out the clock's hands at the bottom of page 86. Then arrange the hands on the clock to show each MotMot's finishing time. Fill in the times on the digital clocks below each MotMot.

Amelia finished the obstacle course at 2:15 p.m.

Brian finished 15 minutes later.

Callie finished 1 hour and 30 minutes after Brian.

Dimitri finished at 15 minutes before 6.

Enid finished at half past 6.

Frank finished 2 hours and 20 minutes after Enid.

Amelia   Brian   Callie   Dimitri   Enid   Frank

LET'S START! GATHER THESE TOOLS AND MATERIALS.

Timer

1–5 sheets of colored construction paper

Scissors (with an adult's help)

Glue

2 paper plates or shoebox lids

10–20 pieces of tube pasta

Crayons

1 marble

LET'S TINKER!

Plan an obstacle course that starts at your front door and ends in your bedroom. **Include** lots of different movements like crawling, hopping, and balancing, and challenges like tossing a toy into a laundry basket. Once you've designed your course, **try** it! **Time** yourself and then see if you can beat your own time.

LET'S MAKE: MINI OBSTACLE COURSE!

1. Cut the paper into strips.

2. Glue each end of the strips to the plate or shoebox lid to create tunnels.

3. Glue the pasta down to create tracks.

4. Write START and FINISH, and draw arrows with a crayon to show the route.

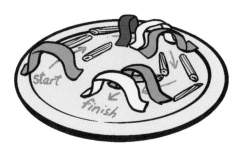

5. Drop a marble in and use a timer to measure how long it takes to complete your mini obstacle course.

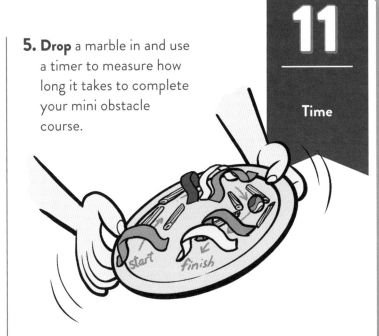

LET'S ENGINEER!

Dimitri has mastered his obstacle course and can finish it lickety-split. Now he wants a challenge!

How can Dimitri modify his obstacle course so it's harder, but also more fun?

Make your home obstacle course or marble obstacle course more difficult and more fun. **Try** changing the route or adding new materials and obstacles. Then **test** it out.

How long does it take you to complete the new course? Longer or shorter than before? Is it harder? Is it more fun? **Challenge** a friend or family member to beat your time.

PROJECT 11: DONE!
Get your sticker!

Money

Write the name and value for each type of coin.

Name: _____

Value: _____

Name: _____

Value: _____

Name: _____

Value: _____

Name: _____

Value: _____

Add the coins using place value and jumping. Include the symbols for dollars ($) or for cents (¢) in your answer.

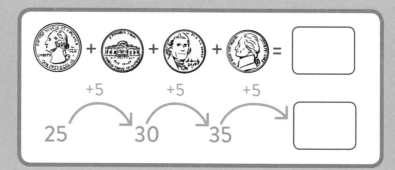

+5   +5   +5

25   30   35

+___   +___

_____   _____

+___   +___   +___   +___   +___

_____   _____   _____   _____   _____

Draw a line from each item on the menu to the matching amount of money.

ICE CREAM 43¢

TACO BOWL 57¢

TURKEY LEG 91¢

FUNNEL CAKE 78¢

What would you buy from Enid's Treat Truck if you had $1.00? Circle your choice!

How would you pay for each item? Write the amount of each coin or bill that you would use to buy each item.

$1.73

$2.15

$1.83

$3.91

Solve each word problem.

Frank has 98¢ and buys a teddy bear in a wagon.

How much money will he have left?

Enid has 50¢ and wants the basket of baskets.

How much money will she have left?

Brian wants a stuffed giraffe. He has one dollar.

How much money will he have left?

Amelia has two dollars. She wants the volleyball.

How much money will she have left?

Do you have some coins? Write your own word problem based on what change you have and what you would like to buy. How much money will you have left?

Circle the money so 3 MotMots each get $1.00. Use each coin only once.

Draw a dollar bill for Frank.

Get the following coins: 4 quarters, 5 dimes, 10 nickels, and 10 pennies. Use the coins to answer each question below.

What is the fewest number of coins necessary to make 62¢?

Draw those coins.

What is the fewest number of coins necessary to make 48¢?

Draw those coins.

What are other ways to make 48¢ using your pennies, nickels, dimes, and quarters?

Draw two other ways.

LET'S START!

GATHER THESE TOOLS AND MATERIALS.

At least 15 pennies, 15 nickels,
15 dimes, and 15 quarters

Cardboard or a cardboard box
(larger than 18 inches by 9 inches)

Tape

Glue

Scissors
(with an adult's help)

Pencil

Newspaper

LET'S TINKER!

Look at and touch your coins,
then brainstorm different ways to
sort them.

How can you sort coins in
different ways?

What is unique about each coin?

LET'S MAKE: COIN-SORTING TRAY!

1. Ask an adult to cut the cardboard into
3 rectangles that are 18 by 3 inches.

2. Place a dime, a penny, a nickel, and a quarter on
the cardboard with space between each one, as
shown below.

3. Draw a rectangle around each coin and ask an adult to cut out the rectangles.

4. Glue the other 2 pieces of cardboard to the sides as the walls of your coin-sorting tray.

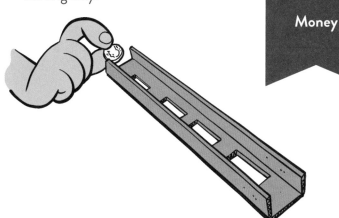

5. Slide your coins over the tray. Does it sort them?

LET'S ENGINEER!

Enid's Treat Truck is so popular that the MotMots are all giving her their piggy banks. Now she has too many coins to sort and count!

If Enid wants to find out how much money she has in quarters, how can she sort out just the quarters?

Modify your coin-sorting tray so you can pour lots of coins into it at once and sort out only the quarters. How much money do you have in quarters?

PROJECT 12: DONE!
Get your sticker!

Data & Graphs

Use the picture graph to answer each question below.

Number of Burgers Eaten	Amelia	Brian	Callie	Dimitri	Enid	Frank
10						
9	🍔					
8	🍔					
7	🍔				🍔	
6	🍔				🍔	
5	🍔	🍔			🍔	🍔
4	🍔	🍔	🍔		🍔	🍔
3	🍔	🍔	🍔		🍔	🍔
2	🍔	🍔	🍔		🍔	🍔
1	🍔	🍔	🍔	🍔	🍔	🍔

How many burgers has Amelia eaten? _____

How many burgers has Dimitri eaten? _____

Which MotMots ate the same number of burgers? _____

How many burgers did Amelia and Enid eat altogether? _____

How many fewer burgers did Callie eat than Brian? _____

Which MotMots ate a combined total of 8 burgers? _____

Use the picture graph to answer each question below.

The MotMots' Favorite Sports

Soccer	
Tennis	
Hockey	
Volleyball	
Bowling	

 = 1 MotMot

What is the most popular sport? _____

What is the least popular sport? _____

How many MotMots like soccer best? _____

How many combined MotMots love volleyball and hockey? _____

How many fewer MotMots like hockey than tennis? _____

How many fewer MotMots like volleyball than bowling? _____

Tally the medals that Brian won.

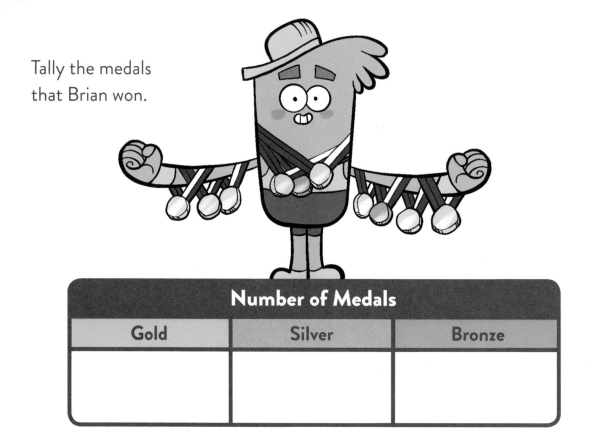

Number of Medals		
Gold	Silver	Bronze

Use the tally chart to draw Brian's medals in each picture graph.

Number of Medals			
6			
5			
4			
3			
2			
1			
	Gold	Silver	Bronze

🏅 = 1 Medal

Gold	
Silver	
Bronze	

🏅 = 1 Medal

Ask 10 friends or family members the following question: Are the baseballs below the same size or is one bigger than the other? Then, in the graph below, color in one space to record each person's response.

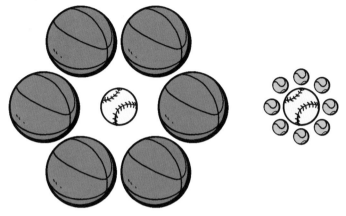

Number of People	Left is bigger	Right is bigger	Same size
10			
9			
8			
7			
6			
5			
4			
3			
2			
1			

Fun fact: The two baseballs are actually the **same size**! Try measuring them to see for yourself.

How many MotMots are participating in each MotMot Olympics event? Look at page 103 and collect the data you need. Then fill in the bar graph.

Number of MotMots				
5				
4				
3				
2				
1				
	Cycling	Fencing	Race Walking	Volleyball

Look carefully at all the MotMots on page 103. How many gold, silver, and bronze medals did they win? Use the space below to create a tally chart.

Gold	
Silver	
Bronze	

LET'S START! GATHER THESE TOOLS AND MATERIALS.

7 pieces of $8\frac{1}{2}$ x 11 paper

Construction paper

15 straws

12 inches of string

Glue or tape

Marker

LET'S TINKER!

Fold 3 different pieces of paper into 3 different shapes and flick them across the room. **Measure** and record the distance for each shape, flicking each 3 times. Did one shape do better than the others?

LET'S MAKE: FLYING FRANK!

1. Fold a piece of paper in half lengthwise.

2. Take a corner and fold it into a triangle. Keep folding until you reach the end.

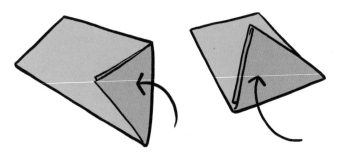

3. Tuck the extra paper into the triangle to secure it.

4. Apply the stickers from page 129 to each side.

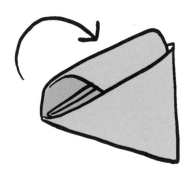

5. Flick this shape 3 times across the room and add the results to the data for the three shapes you tried before.

LET'S ENGINEER!

Frankball is the MotMots' favorite pastime. The only problem is that no one ever remembers the score!

How can the MotMots keep score?

Use the straws and string to create different-size targets for Frank to fly through or land on. **Ask** friends or family members to play—you get one point for every successful flick. Then **create** a scoreboard to keep score as you play. What is the best way to label the scoreboard or count your points?

PROJECT 13: DONE!
Get your sticker!

Shape Attributes

Fill in the missing information in the chart below.

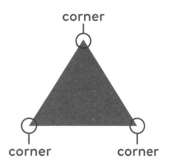

corner

corner   corner

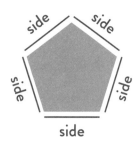

side side

side   side

side

Shape	Name	Number of Corners	Number of Sides
●		O	O
			3
■			
	rectangle		
▰	trapezoid		
	pentagon		
⬡			

Quadrilaterals have four sides. Circle the quadrilaterals.

Fill in the missing information for each shape.

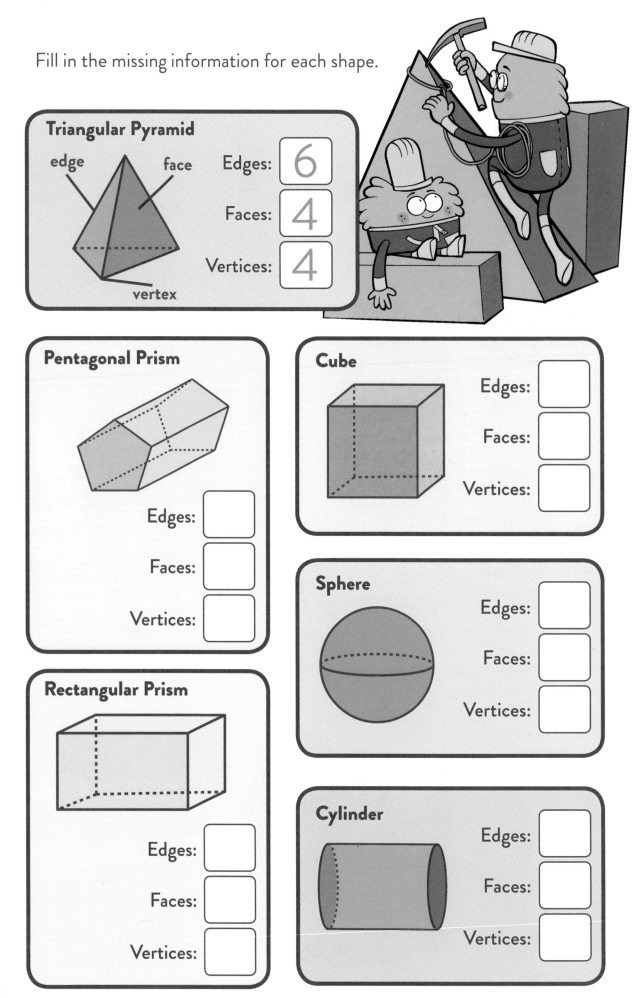

Triangular Pyramid

edge   face

Edges: 6

Faces: 4

Vertices: 4

vertex

Pentagonal Prism

Edges:

Faces:

Vertices:

Cube

Edges:

Faces:

Vertices:

Sphere

Edges:

Faces:

Vertices:

Rectangular Prism

Edges:

Faces:

Vertices:

Cylinder

Edges:

Faces:

Vertices:

Read the clues and draw each shape.

Amelia's favorite 2-dimensional shape has 4 corners and 4 equal sides.

Dimitri's favorite 3-dimensional shape has 2 edges and 2 faces.

Enid's favorite 2-dimensional shape has no sides.

Frank's favorite 2-dimensional shape has 3 corners.

Color the image using the key below.

Triangles: Blue
Quadrilaterals: Pink
Pentagons: Green
Hexagons: Orange

Draw a line to guide Brian through the maze to the exit.

Brian can only step on shapes that have 1 more or 1 less side than the previous shape he stepped on.

Brian cannot move diagonally.

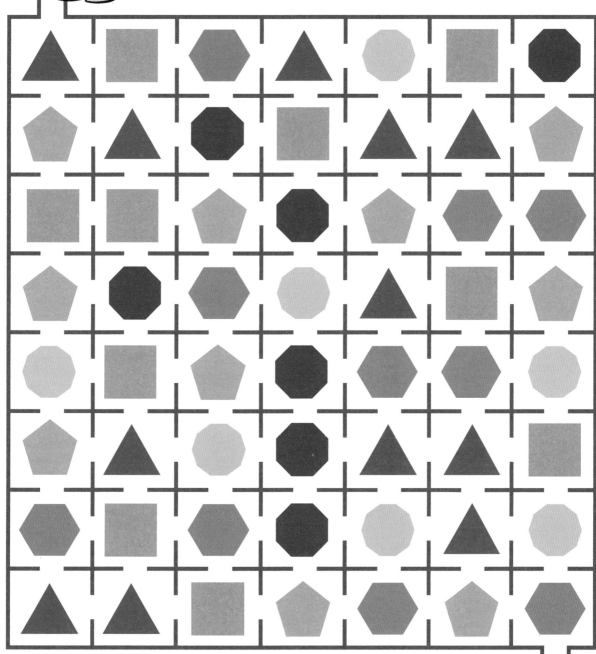

EXIT!

LET'S START!

10 pipe cleaners

5 plastic shopping bags

Scissors
(with an adult's help)

Paper clips

4 feet of string

Tape

6 coins

LET'S TINKER!

Fold the pipe cleaners into different 2-dimensional shapes. Then **make** 3-dimensional shapes. Can you make shapes by combining other shapes? Or how about making 3-dimensional shapes by combining 2-dimensional shapes?

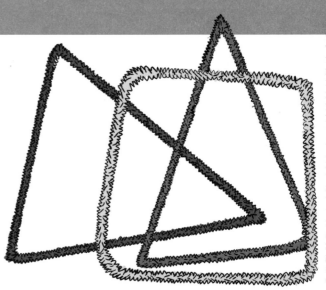

LET'S MAKE: PARACHUTE!

1. **Cut** a cone shape out of the corner of a plastic shopping bag.

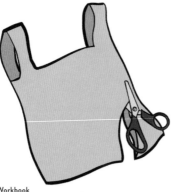

2. **Use** a straightened paper clip to punch holes into four points along the edge. **Punch** the holes so there is equal distance between them.

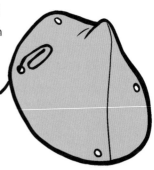

3. Thread a piece of string through each hole and tie it. If the bag tears, **use** tape to reinforce the holes.

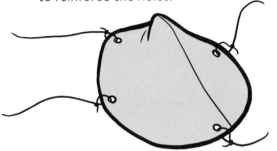

4. Tie the strings to a pipe cleaner.

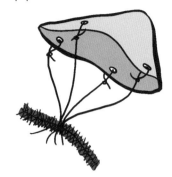

5. Wrap the pipe cleaner around a coin.

6. Test your parachute!

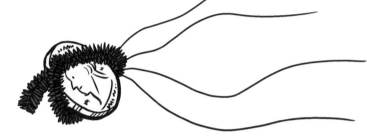

LET'S ENGINEER!

Now that the MotMots have parachutes, they are ready to go skydiving. But they want to float in the air as long as possible.

How can each MotMot float for a longer amount of time?

Apply the MotMot stickers from page 129 to some coins. **Drop** each MotMot with a parachute, and time how long it takes them to get to the ground. How could you modify each parachute so it stays in the air longer? **Try** some different designs and shapes, then time the skydives! Which design floats the longest?

PROJECT 14: DONE!
Get your sticker!

Geometry

Draw lines to divide each rectangle into parts that are the same size. Then count the number of parts.

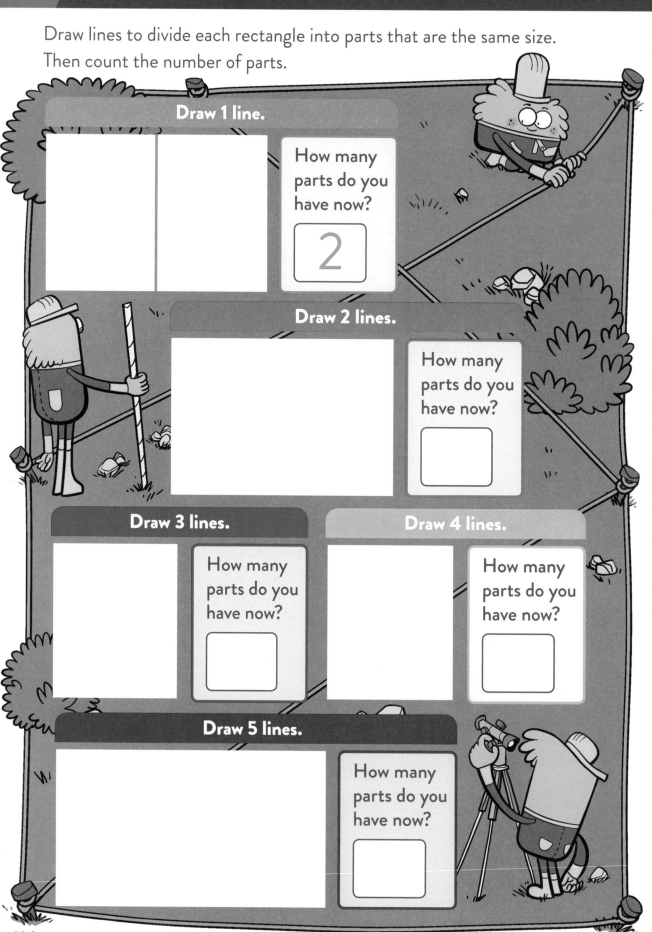

Draw 1 line.

How many parts do you have now?

2

Draw 2 lines.

How many parts do you have now?

Draw 3 lines.

How many parts do you have now?

Draw 4 lines.

How many parts do you have now?

Draw 5 lines.

How many parts do you have now?

Color in the parts of each beam.

1 part out of 2

2 parts out of 3

2 parts out of 5

3 parts out of 8

4 parts out of 6

How many parts of each shape are missing?
Fill in each sentence. Then read it aloud.

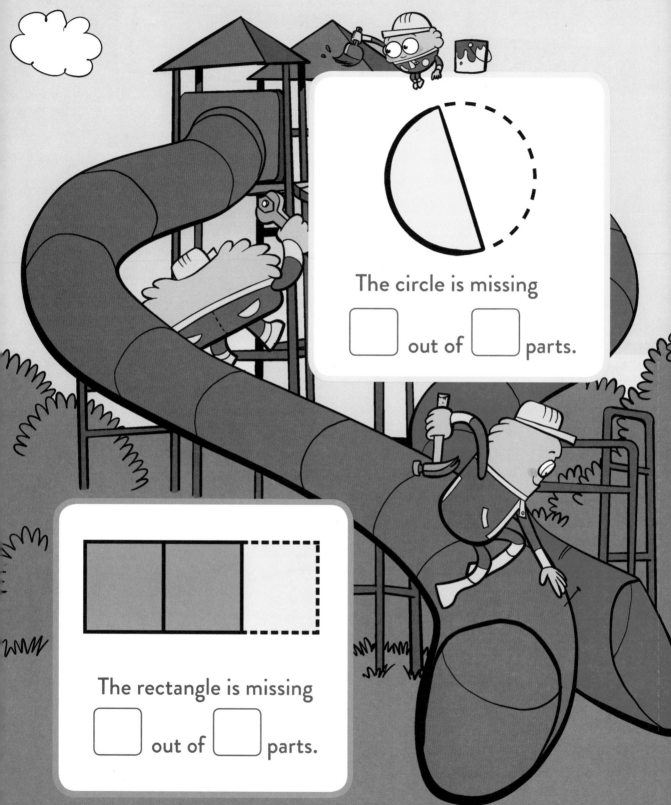

The circle is missing

[ ] out of [ ] parts.

The rectangle is missing

[ ] out of [ ] parts.

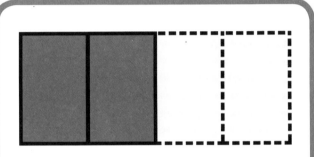

The circle is missing [ ] out of [ ] parts.

The rectangle is missing [ ] out of [ ] parts.

The rectangle is missing [ ] out of [ ] parts.

Match the shape to each description.

1 part out of 3
or
one-third
is white

1 part out of 2
or
one-half
is white

1 part out of 4
or
one-fourth
is white

3 parts out of 4
or
three-fourths
is white

2 parts out of 3
or
two-thirds
is white

Color the parts of each shape as labeled.

One-fourth

One-half

Two-thirds

Two-fifths

One-third

Two-thirds

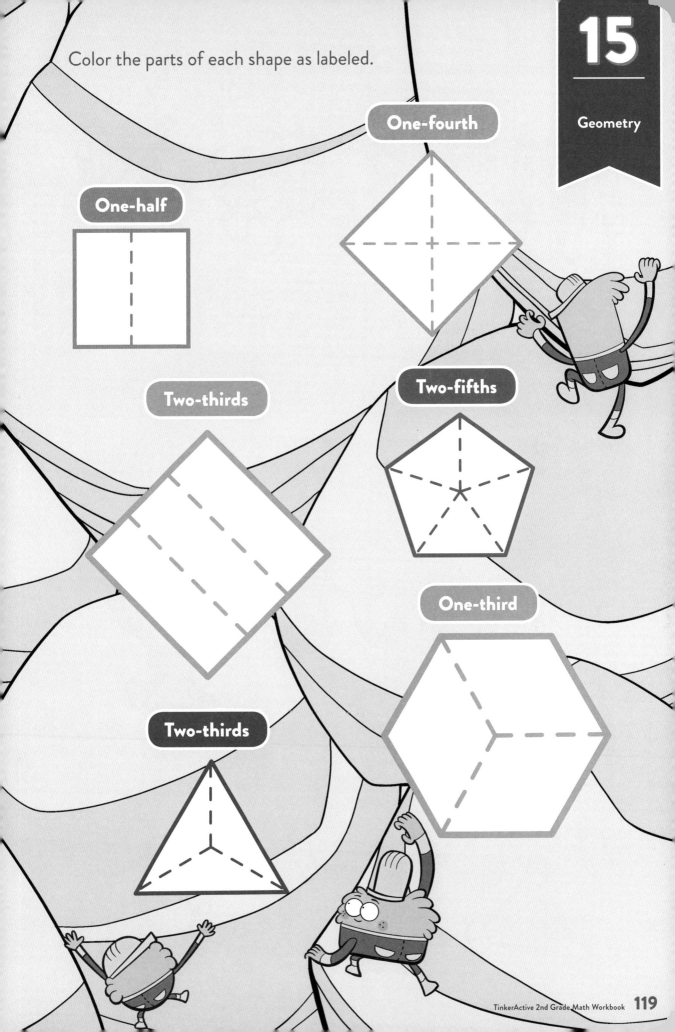

LET'S START!

Craft sticks

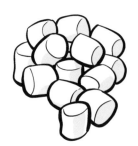

Toothpicks

100 small marshmallows

Small figurines or or stuffed animals

LET'S TINKER!

Explore the materials to see how sturdy they are. How can you combine the materials to make them sturdier? What shapes and combinations are the strongest?

LET'S MAKE: MARSHMALLOW SHAPES!

1. Using toothpicks, **create** the base shapes of a square, a triangle, and a pentagon.

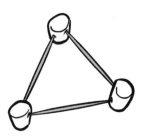
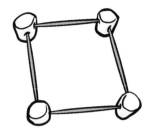
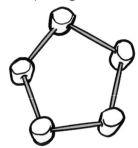

2. Make more of the base shapes from step 1 and combine them to make pyramids or cubes.

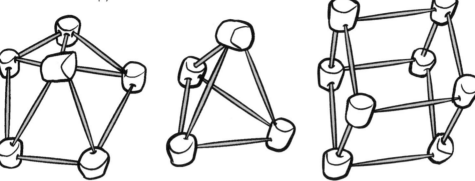

What other 2- and 3-dimensional shapes can you make?

LET'S ENGINEER!

The MotMots want to make a jungle gym to climb on at the playground, but they don't know what the strongest shape is.

How can the MotMots test the strength of different shapes?

Make a structure with your materials that reaches up to 12 inches using only one kind of shape. Then **make** another structure using another kind of shape. **Place** your stuffed animals or figurines on each structure to test its strength. Which shape is strongest?

ANSWER KEY

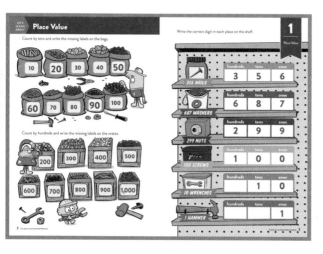

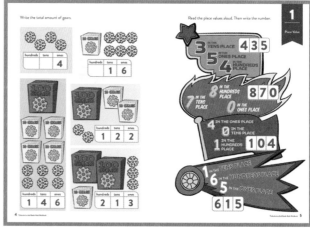

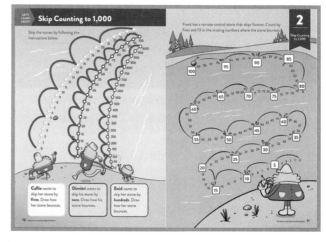

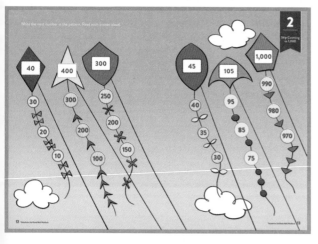

Comparing Numbers

Dimitri and Enid made a game called Less Than, Greater Than, Mot, Mot, Mot! Play it by yourself, or with a friend. Follow the directions, and when you reach each item, shout "MOT! MOT! MOT!"

Look around you. Can you touch something **SOFT** by taking less than three steps? Race to it and shout, "MOT, MOT, MOT!"

Now touch something **SHINY** in less than 2 hops.

Can you touch something **STRIPED** in greater than 9 skips?

Touch something **BIGGER** than you in less than 5 backward steps.

Can you touch something **BLUE** in greater than 12 side steps?

Read each word problem. Then fill in the sentences and circle the >, <, or =.

Brian and Callie went to the cheese shop. Callie put 13 wedge-shaped cheeses into her basket. Brian took 20 wedges.

Brian has **20** wedges of cheese. **>** Callie has **13** wedges of cheese.

Next, Brian saw a carton of 300 gooey cheeses. It smelled like feet, so he give it to Callie. He took 125 gooey cheeses for himself.

Brian has **125** gooey cheeses. **<** Callie has **300** gooey cheeses.

Then Callie added her favorite pouch of 50 mini wheels to her basket. And Brian picked up 50 mini wheels.

Brian has **50** mini wheels. **=** Callie has **50** mini wheels.

At the last moment, Callie went back and got 3 bags of shredded cheese. Brian doesn't like shredded cheese, so he didn't get any.

Brian has **0** bags of shredded cheese. **<** Callie has **3** bags of shredded cheese.

Frank's pet alligator is hungry! Which containers have more food?

Compare the number on each container. Then write >, <, or = in each space.

747 **>** 724

537 **<** 812

981 **=** 981

743 **>** 643

619 **<** 632

15 **=** 15

501 **>** 491

113 **=** 113

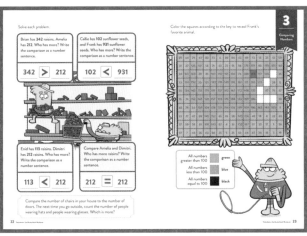

Solve each problem.

Brian has **342** raisins. Amelia has **212**. Who has more? Write the comparison as a number sentence.

342 **>** 212

Callie has **102** sunflower seeds, and Frank has **931** sunflower seeds. Who has more? Write the comparison as a number sentence.

102 **<** 931

Enid has **113** raisins. Dimitri has **212** raisins. Who has more? Write the comparison as a number sentence.

113 **<** 212

Compare Amelia and Dimitri. Who has more raisins? Write the comparison as a number sentence.

212 **=** 212

Compare the number of chairs in your house to the number of doors. The next time you go outside, count the number of people wearing hats and people wearing glasses. Which is more?

Color the squares according to the key to reveal Frank's favorite animal.

All numbers greater than 100 — green
All numbers less than 100 — blue
All numbers equal to 100 — black

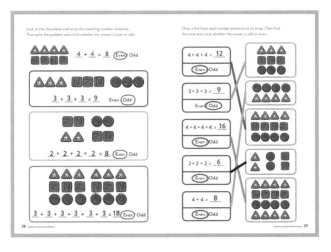

Even & Odd

Callie and Brian are making chocolate bars. Color the squares in the chocolate mold to represent each number. Then circle whether the number is even or odd.

6 — Odd / Even
5 — Odd / Even
11 — Odd / Even
10 — Odd / Even
12 — Odd / Even
9 — Odd / Even

Follow the directions to reveal Brian's favorite filling for chocolates.

Color the squares with even numbers between 10 and 30 **red**.
Color the squares with odd numbers between 30 and 50 **green**.
Color the squares with even numbers between 51 and 60 **black**.

A number whose last digit is 0, 2, 4, 6, or 8 is even. All other numbers are odd.

Look at the chocolates and write the matching number sentence. Then solve the problem and circle whether the answer is even or odd.

4 + **4** = **8**   (Even) Odd

3 + **3** + **3** = **9**   Even (Odd)

2 + **2** + **2** + **2** = **8**   (Even) Odd

3 + **3** + **3** + **3** + **3** + **3** = **18**   (Even) Odd

Draw a line from each number sentence to its array. Then find the total and circle whether the answer is odd or even.

4 + 4 + 4 = **12**   (Even) Odd

3 + 3 + 3 = **9**   Even (Odd)

4 + 4 + 4 + 4 = **16**   (Even) Odd

2 + 2 + 2 = **6**   (Even) Odd

4 + 4 = **8**   (Even) Odd

Answers will vary.

How many months till your birthday?		Even	Odd
How many chairs do you see right now?		Even	Odd
What is your age plus 7?		Even	Odd
How many steps are between your kitchen and the bathroom?		Even	Odd
What is the number of kids in your class plus 4?		Even	Odd
How many red objects can you count around you now?		Even	Odd

Answers will vary.

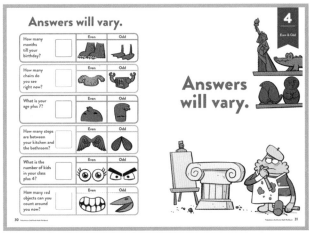

Addition & Subtraction

You can solve a subtraction problem by thinking of the related addition problem. Solve each set of problems.

$\begin{array}{r} 7 \\ -3 \\ \hline 4 \end{array}$ $\begin{array}{r} 3 \\ +4 \\ \hline 7 \end{array}$

$\begin{array}{r} 11 \\ -6 \\ \hline 5 \end{array}$ $\begin{array}{r} 6 \\ +5 \\ \hline 11 \end{array}$

$\begin{array}{r} 14 \\ -6 \\ \hline 8 \end{array}$ $\begin{array}{r} 6 \\ +8 \\ \hline 14 \end{array}$

$\begin{array}{r} 13 \\ -8 \\ \hline 5 \end{array}$ $\begin{array}{r} 8 \\ +5 \\ \hline 13 \end{array}$

$\begin{array}{r} 15 \\ -9 \\ \hline 6 \end{array}$ $\begin{array}{r} 9 \\ +6 \\ \hline 15 \end{array}$

$\begin{array}{r} 16 \\ -9 \\ \hline 7 \end{array}$ $\begin{array}{r} 9 \\ +7 \\ \hline 16 \end{array}$

Use the crosshouse chart below to solve the problems on the next page. Put your finger on the first number and then add or subtract by moving your finger by tens and then by ones. Fill in the sentences and write your answer.

1	2	3	4	5	6	7	8	9	10
11	12	13	14	15	16	17	18	19	20
21	22	23	24	25	26	27	28	29	30
31	32	33	34	35	36	37	38	39	40
41	42	43	44	45	46	47	48	49	50
51	52	53	54	55	56	57	58	59	60
61	62	63	64	65	66	67	68	69	70
71	72	73	74	75	76	77	78	79	80
81	82	83	84	85	86	87	88	89	90
91	92	93	94	95	96	97	98	99	100

43 + 17 = 60
- Start at 43.
- Jump **10** spaces forward.
- Then move **7** more spaces forward.

74 − 19 = 55
- Start at 74.
- Jump **10** spaces backward.
- Then move **9** more spaces backward.

25 + 28 = 53
- Start at 25.
- Jump **20** spaces forward.
- Then move **8** more spaces forward.

93 − 19 = 74
- Start at 93.
- Jump **10** spaces backward.
- Then move **9** more spaces backward.

18 + 53 = 71
- Start at 18.
- Jump **50** spaces forward.
- Then move **3** more spaces forward.

55 − 26 = 29
- Start at 55.
- Jump **20** spaces backward.
- Then move **6** more spaces backward.

46 + 16 = 62
- Start at 46.
- Jump **10** spaces forward.
- Then move **6** more spaces forward.

84 − 77 = 7
- Start at 84.
- Jump **70** spaces backward.
- Then move **7** more spaces backward.

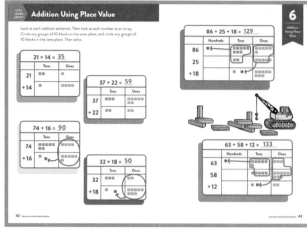

Addition Using Place Value

Look at each addition sentence. Then look at each number as an array. Circle any groups of 10 blocks in the ones place, and circle any groups of 10 blocks in the tens place. Then solve.

$21 + 14 = 35$

$37 + 22 = 59$

$74 + 16 = 90$

$32 + 18 = 50$

$86 + 25 + 18 = 129$

$63 + 58 + 12 = 133$

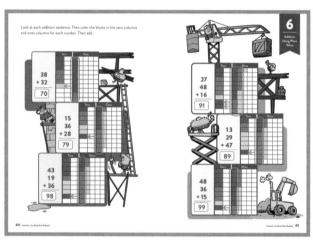

Look at each addition sentence. Then color the blocks in the tens columns and ones columns for each number. Then add.

$38 + 32 = 70$

$15 + 36 + 28 = 79$

$43 + 19 + 36 = 98$

$27 + 48 + 16 = 91$

$13 + 29 + 47 = 89$

$48 + 36 + 15 = 99$

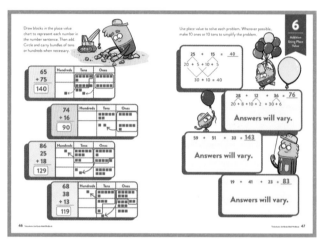

Draw blocks in the place value chart to represent each number in the number sentence. Then add. Circle and carry bundles of tens or hundreds when necessary.

$65 + 75 = 140$

$74 + 16 = 90$

$86 + 25 + 18 = 129$

$68 + 38 + 13 = 119$

Use place value to solve each problem. Wherever possible, make 10 ones or 10 tens to simplify the problem.

$25 + 15 = 40$
$20 + 5 + 10 + 5 = 30 + 10 = 40$

$28 + 12 + 36 = 76$
$20 + 8 + 10 + 2 + 30 + 6 =$

Answers will vary.

$59 + 51 + 33 = 143$

Answers will vary.

$19 + 41 + 23 = 83$

Answers will vary.

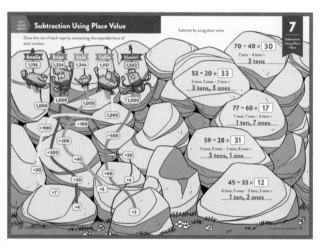

Subtraction Using Place Value

Draw the rest of each rope by connecting the expanded form of each number.

Amelia 1,156
Brian 1,324
Enid 1,246
Callie 1,937
Dimitri 1,542

Subtract by using place value.

$70 - 40 = 30$
7 tens − 4 tens = 3 tens

$53 - 20 = 33$
5 tens, 3 ones − 2 tens = 3 tens, 3 ones

$77 - 60 = 17$
7 tens, 7 ones − 6 tens = 1 ten, 7 ones

$59 - 28 = 31$
5 tens, 9 ones − 2 tens, 8 ones = 3 tens, 1 one

$45 - 33 = 12$
4 tens, 5 ones − 3 tens, 3 ones = 1 ten, 2 ones

Subtract by using the expanded number form and jumping hundreds, tens, and ones.

$34 - 11 = 23$

$48 - 35 = 13$

$68 - 17 = 51$

$86 - 48 = 38$

$643 - 126 = 517$

$427 - 213 = 214$

$866 - 542 = 324$

$981 - 580 = 401$

Use the place value chart to solve each problem.

$39 - 12 = 27$
$58 - 26 = 32$
$76 - 43 = 33$
$98 - 25 = 73$

The MotMots are packing their backpacks for a nature hike! Draw a place value chart to solve each word problem.

Enid decided to pack 183 of her favorite cotton balls. But then she decided she didn't need 72 of them, so she unpacked them. How many does she have packed?
$183 - 72 = 111$

Frank packed 175 egg sandwiches, but he ate 30 of them. How many does he have left?
$175 - 30 = 145$

Dimitri packed 432 rubber bands. Callie packed 100 fewer. How many did Callie pack?
$432 - 100 = 332$

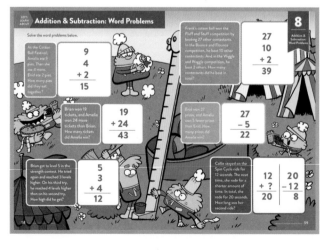

Addition & Subtraction: Word Problems

Solve the word problems below.

At the Cotton Ball Festival, Amelia ate 9 pies. Then she ate 4 more. And she ate 2 yes. How many pies did she eat together?
$9 + 4 + 2 = 15$

Brian won 19 tickets, and Amelia won 24 more tickets than Brian. How many tickets did Amelia win?
$19 + 24 = 43$

Brian got to level 5 in the strength contest. He tried again and reached 3 levels higher. On his third try, he reached 4 levels higher than on his second try. How high did he get?
$5 + 3 + 4 = 12$

Frank's cotton ball won the Fluff and Stuff competition by beating 27 other contestants. In the Bounce and Flounce competition, he beat 10 other contestants. And in the Wiggle and Waggle competition, he beat 2 others. How many contestants did he beat in total?
$27 + 10 + 2 = 39$

Enid won 27 prizes, and Amelia won 5 fewer prizes than Enid. How many prizes did Amelia win?
$27 - 5 = 22$

Callie stayed on the Spin Cycle ride for 12 seconds. The next time, she rode for a shorter amount of time. In total, she rode for 20 seconds. How long was her second ride?
$12 + ? = 20$ $20 - 12 = 8$

Read the story. As you read, tally the costume photos on page 45 by drawing circles (O) to add or crossing circles out (⊘) to subtract.

Dimitri ran around the Cotton Ball Festival to take photos of all the different costumes. He saw **10** cowboy cotton balls in the cafeteria and **2** more by the water fountain.

He spotted **14** astronaut cotton balls on the trampolines. Then **4** more arrived. But then **10** of them took off their helmets and they were actually pirates!

Another **12** pirates were standing by the donut truck, along with **4** more cowboys.

Finally, in the dance hall at the Cotton Ball, he saw **7** cowboys, **2** pirates, **7** ninjas, and **1** astronaut.

That was when Dimitri saw that his camera's battery was almost dead. As he replaced the battery, he accidentally erased pictures of **10** cowboys and **3** astronauts.

Can you write your own word problem using cotton balls?

By the end of the night, how many pictures of each costume did he have?

| cowboys | 13 | ninjas | 7 |
| astronauts | 6 | pirates | 24 |

8 — Addition & Subtraction Word Problems

Fill in the number sentences to solve. Then draw a line from each MotMot to the prize they can get using all their tickets.

Dimitri won **73** tickets from the carnival games. He gave **20** away. Then he won another **17**.
Step 1: 73 − 20 = __53__
Step 2: __53__ + 17 = __70__

Frank won **84** tickets for his prize cotton ball. He won another **11** for the dance competition. Then he lost **20** through a hole in his pocket.
Step 1: 84 + 11 = __95__
Step 2: __95__ − 20 = __75__

Callie won **81** tickets. She accidentally lost **30** of them when she went on the Spin Cycle ride. Then she won another **23**.
Step 1: 81 − 30 = __51__
Step 2: __51__ + 23 = __74__

Enid won only **9** tickets because she could not see over the counter. Amelia gave her **65** tickets to make her feel better. But **40** of those tickets were covered in cherry pie and couldn't be used.
Step 1: 9 + 65 = __74__
Step 2: 74 − 40 = __34__

Frank   Callie   Dimitri   Enid

8 — Addition & Subtraction Word Problems

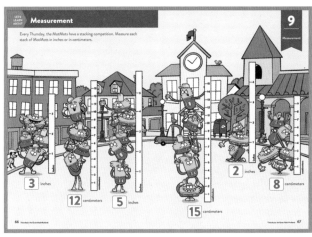

LET'S LEARN ABOUT
Measurement

Every Thursday, the MotMots have a stacking competition. Measure each stack of MotMots in inches or in centimeters.

3 inches
12 centimeters
5 inches
15 centimeters
2 inches
8 centimeters

9 — Measurement

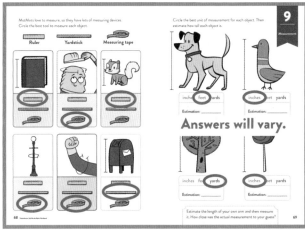

MotMots love to measure, so they have lots of measuring devices. Circle the best tool to measure each object.

Ruler   Yardstick   Measuring tape

Circle the best unit of measurement for each object. Then estimate how tall each object is.

inches **feet** yards   Estimation: _____
inches feet yards   Estimation: _____

Answers will vary.

inches feet **yards**   Estimation: _____
inches **feet** yards   Estimation: _____

Estimate the length of your own arm and then measure it. How close was the actual measurement to your guess?

9 — Measurement

Put your hand on the page and trace around it. Then use a ruler to measure each finger in inches and in centimeters. Write your measurements next to each finger. Then measure the length of your whole hand in inches and in centimeters and write your measurements below.

Answers will vary.

My hand is _____ inches or _____ centimeters long.

Put your foot on the page and trace around it. Then measure the length of your foot in inches and in centimeters. Write your measurements below.

Answers will vary.

My foot is _____ inches or _____ centimeters long.

9 — Measurement

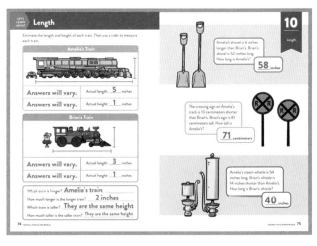

LET'S LEARN ABOUT
Length

Estimate the length and height of each train. Then use a ruler to measure each train.

Amelia's Train
Answers will vary. — Actual length: __5__ inches
Answers will vary. — Actual height: __1__ inches

Brian's Train
Answers will vary. — Actual length: __3__ inches
Answers will vary. — Actual height: __1__ inches

Which train is longer? __Amelia's train__
How much longer is the longer train? __2 inches__
Which train is taller? __They are the same height__
How much taller is the taller train? __They are the same height__

Amelia's shovel is 6 inches longer than Brian's. Brian's shovel is 52 inches long. How long is Amelia's?
__58__ inches

The crossing sign on Amelia's track is 10 centimeters shorter than Brian's. Brian's sign is 81 centimeters tall. How tall is Amelia's?
__71__ centimeters

Amelia's steam whistle is 54 inches long. Brian's whistle is 14 inches shorter than Amelia's. How long is Brian's whistle?
__40__ inches

10 — Length

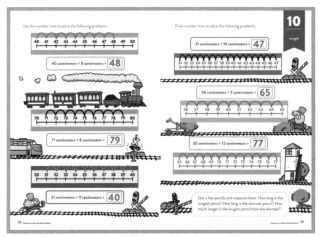

Use the number lines to solve the following problems.

40 41 42 43 44 45 46 47 48 49 50
40 centimeters + 8 centimeters = 48

70 71 72 73 74 75 76 77 78 79 80
71 centimeters + 8 centimeters = 79

30 31 32 33 34 35 36 37 38 39 40
31 centimeters + 9 centimeters = 40

Draw number lines to solve the following problems.

31 32 33 34 35 36 37 38 39 40 41 42 43 44 45 46 47
31 centimeters + 16 centimeters = 47

56 57 58 59 60 61 62 63 64 65
56 centimeters + 9 centimeters = 65

65 66 67 68 69 70 71 72 73 74 75 76 77
65 centimeters + 12 centimeters = 77

Get a few pencils and measure them. How long is the longest pencil? How long is the shortest pencil? How much longer is the longest pencil than the shortest?

10 — Length

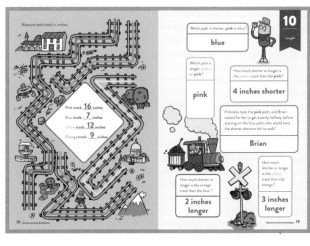

Measure each track in inches.

Which path is shorter, pink or blue?
blue

Which path is longer, yellow or pink?
pink

How much shorter or longer is the yellow track than the pink?
4 inches shorter

If Amelia took the pink path, and Brian waited for her to get exactly halfway before starting on the blue path, who would have the shorter distance left to walk?
Brian

Pink track: **16** inches
Blue track: **20** inches
Yellow track: **12** inches
Orange track: **9** inches

How much shorter or longer is the orange track than the blue?
2 inches longer

How much shorter or longer is the yellow track than the orange?
3 inches longer

10 — Length

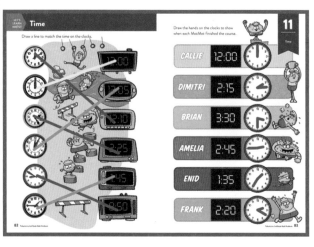

Time — 11

Draw a line to match the time on the clocks.

Draw the hands on the clocks to show when each MotMot finished the course.

CALLIE	12:00
DIMITRI	2:15
BRIAN	3:30
AMELIA	2:45
ENID	1:35
FRANK	2:20

11 — Time

Count by fives to tell the time. Then fill in the missing numbers in each sentence.

The clock shows **30** minutes after **3** o'clock.
It's **3 : 3 0**

The clock shows **15** minutes after **4** o'clock.
It's **4 : 1 5**

The clock shows **45** minutes after **2** o'clock.
It's **2 : 4 5**

The clock shows **15** minutes after **9** o'clock.
It's **9 : 1 5**

The clock shows **30** minutes after **7** o'clock.
It's **7 : 3 0**

When do you do each activity? Draw hands on the clock. Then fill in the missing time in the sentence, as well as a.m. or p.m.

Answers will vary.

I wake up at ___ : ___   I eat breakfast at ___ : ___
I have recess at ___ : ___   I go home at ___ : ___
I eat dinner at ___ : ___   I go to bed at ___ : ___

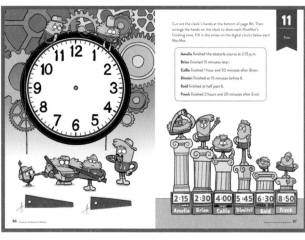

11 — Time

Cut out the clock's hands at the bottom of page 86. Then arrange the hands on the clock to show each MotMot's finishing time. Fill in the times on the digital clocks below each MotMot.

Amelia finished the obstacle course at 2:15 p.m.
Brian finished 15 minutes later.
Callie finished 1 hour and 30 minutes after Brian.
Dimitri finished at 15 minutes before 6.
Enid finished at half past 6.
Frank finished 2 hours and 20 minutes after Enid.

| 2:15 | 2:30 | 4:00 | 5:45 | 6:30 | 8:50 |
| Amelia | Brian | Callie | Dimitri | Enid | Frank |

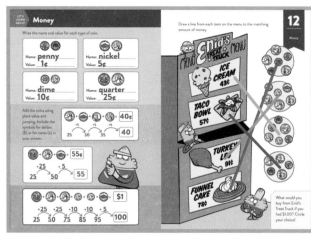

Money — 12

Write the name and value for each type of coin.

Name: **penny** Value: **1¢**
Name: **nickel** Value: **5¢**
Name: **dime** Value: **10¢**
Name: **quarter** Value: **25¢**

Add the coins using place value and jumping. Include the symbols for dollars ($) or for cents (¢) in your answer.

+5 +5 +5 → **40¢**
25 30 35 40

+25 +5 → **55¢**
25 50 55

+25 +25 +10 +10 +5 → **$1**
25 50 75 85 95 100

Draw a line from each item on the menu to the matching amount of money.

Enid's Treat Truck Menu
ICE CREAM 43¢
TACO BOWL 57¢
TURKEY LEG 91¢
FUNNEL CAKE 78¢

What would you buy from Enid's Treat Truck if you had $1.00? Circle your choice!

12 — Money

How would you pay for each item? Write the amount of each coin or bill that you would use to buy each item.

$1.73 — **Answers will vary.**
$2.15 — **Answers will vary.**
$1.83 — **Answers will vary.**
$3.91 — **Answers will vary.**

Solve each word problem.

Frank has 98¢ and buys a teddy bear in a wagon. How much money will he have left? **23¢**

Enid has 50¢ and wants the basket of baskets. How much money will she have left? **13¢**

Brian wants a stuffed giraffe. He has one dollar. How much money will he have left? **20¢**

Amelia has two dollars. She wants the volleyball. How much money will she have left? **$1.00**

Do you have some coins? Write your own word problem based on what change you have and what you would like to buy. How much money will you have left?

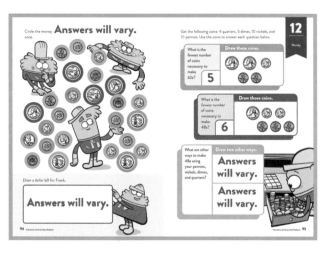

12 — Money

Circle the money **Answers will vary.** once.

Draw a dollar bill for Frank.

Answers will vary.

Get the following coins: 4 quarters, 5 dimes, 10 nickels, and 10 pennies. Use the coins to answer each question below.

What is the fewest number of coins necessary to make 62¢? **5**   Draw those coins.

What is the fewest number of coins necessary to make 48¢? **6**   Draw those coins.

What are other ways to make 48¢ using your pennies, nickels, dimes, and quarters? Draw two other ways.
Answers will vary.
Answers will vary.

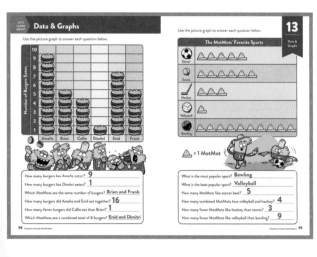

Data & Graphs — 13

Use the picture graph to answer each question below.

Number of Burgers Eaten — Amelia, Brian, Callie, Dimitri, Enid, Frank

How many burgers has Amelia eaten? **9**
How many burgers has Dimitri eaten? **1**
Which MotMots ate the same number of burgers? **Brian and Frank**
How many burgers did Amelia and Enid eat together? **16**
How many fewer burgers did Callie eat than Brian? **1**
Which MotMots ate a combined total of 8 burgers? **Enid and Dimitri**

Use the picture graph to answer each question below.

The MotMots' Favorite Sports
Soccer, Tennis, Hockey, Volleyball, Bowling

△ = 1 MotMot

What is the most popular sport? **Bowling**
What is the least popular sport? **Volleyball**
How many MotMots like soccer best? **5**
How many combined MotMots love volleyball and hockey? **4**
How many fewer MotMots like hockey than tennis? **3**
How many fewer MotMots like volleyball than bowling? **9**

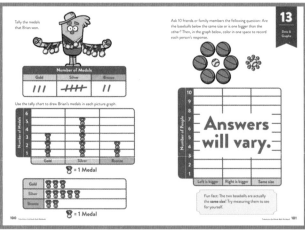

13 — Data & Graphs

Tally the medals that Brian won.

Number of Medals		
Gold	Silver	Bronze
III	‖‖‖	II

Use the tally chart to draw Brian's medals in each picture graph.

Number of Medals — Gold, Silver, Bronze
🏅 = 1 Medal

Gold	🏅🏅🏅
Silver	🏅🏅🏅🏅🏅
Bronze	🏅🏅
🏅 = 1 Medal

Ask 10 friends or family members the following question: Are the baseballs below the same size or is one bigger than the other? Then, in the graph below, color in one space to record each person's response.

Number of People
Answers will vary.
Left is bigger   Right is bigger   Same size

Fun fact: The two baseballs are actually the same size! Try measuring them to see for yourself.

How many MatMots are participating in this MatMot Olympics event? Look at page 103 and collect the data you need. Then fill in the bar graph.

Number of MatMots: 5, 4, 3, 2, 1 — Cycling, Fencing, Race Walking, Volleyball

Look carefully at all the MatMots. How many gold, silver, and bronze medals did they win? Use the space below to create a tally chart.

Gold	///
Silver	///
Bronze	////

102   103

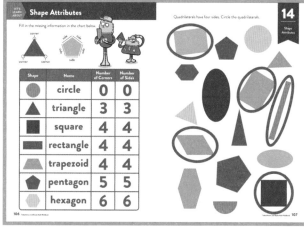

Shape Attributes

Fill in the missing information in the chart below.

corner / side

Shape	Name	Number of Corners	Number of Sides
circle	circle	0	0
triangle	triangle	3	3
square	square	4	4
rectangle	rectangle	4	4
trapezoid	trapezoid	4	4
pentagon	pentagon	5	5
hexagon	hexagon	6	6

Quadrilaterals have four sides. Circle the quadrilaterals.

106   107

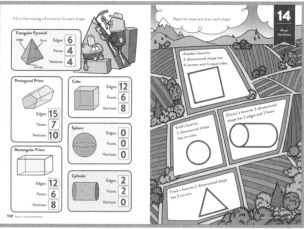

Fill in the missing information for each shape.

Triangular Pyramid — Edges: 6, Faces: 4, Vertices: 4

Pentagonal Prism — Edges: 15, Faces: 7, Vertices: 10

Rectangular Prism — Edges: 12, Faces: 6, Vertices: 8

Cube — Edges: 12, Faces: 6, Vertices: 8

Sphere — Edges: 0, Faces: 0, Vertices: 0

Cylinder — Edges: 2, Faces: 2, Vertices: 0

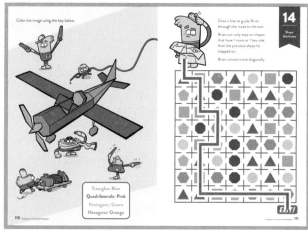

Read the clues and draw each shape.

Amelia's favorite 2-dimensional shape has 4 corners and 4 equal sides.

Enid's favorite 2-dimensional shape has no sides.

Dimitri's favorite 3-dimensional shape has 2 edges and 2 faces.

Frank's favorite 2-dimensional shape has 3 corners.

108

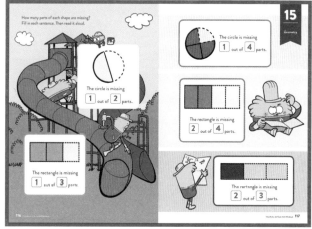

Color the image using the key below.

Triangles: Blue
Quadrilaterals: Pink
Pentagons: Green
Hexagons: Orange

Draw a line to guide Brian through the maze to the exit.

Brian can only step on shapes that have 1 more or 1 less side than the previous shape he stepped on.

Brian cannot move diagonally.

EXIT!

110   111

Geometry

Answers will vary.

same size.

Draw 1 line. How many parts do you have now? 2

Draw 2 lines. How many parts do you have now? 3

Draw 3 lines. How many parts do you have now? 4

Draw 4 lines. How many parts do you have now? 5

Draw 5 lines. How many parts do you have now? 6

Color in the parts of each beam.

1 part out of 2

2 parts out of 3

2 parts out of 5

3 parts out of 8

4 parts out of 6

114   115

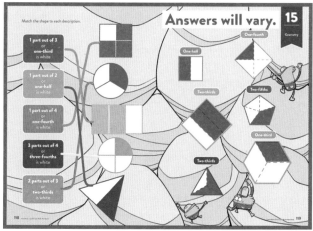

How many parts of each shape are missing? Fill in each sentence. Then read it aloud.

The circle is missing 1 out of 2 parts.

The circle is missing 1 out of 4 parts.

The rectangle is missing 2 out of 4 parts.

The rectangle is missing 1 out of 3 parts.

The rectangle is missing 2 out of 3 parts.

116   117

Match the shape to each description.

Answers will vary.

1 part out of 3 or one-third is white

1 part out of 2 or one-half is white

1 part out of 4 or one-fourth is white

3 parts out of 4 or three-fourths is white

2 parts out of 3 or two-thirds is white

One-fourth · One-half · Two-thirds · Two-fifths · One-third · Two-thirds

118   119

Odd Dot
175 Fifth Avenue
New York, NY 10010
OddDot.com

ISBN: 978-1-250-30723-1

WRITER   Enil Sidat

ILLUSTRATOR   Les McClaine

EDUCATIONAL CONSULTANT   Lindsay Frevert

CHARACTER DESIGNER   Anna-Maria Jung

COVER ILLUSTRATOR   Anna-Maria Jung

BACK COVER ILLUSTRATOR   Chad Thomas

BADGE EMBROIDERER   El Patcha

INTERIOR DESIGNER   Tae Won Yu

COVER DESIGNERS   Carolyn Bahar and Colleen AF Venable

EDITOR   Nathalie Le Du

Our books may be purchased in bulk for promotional, educational, or business use. Please contact your local bookseller or the Macmillan Corporate and Premium Sales Department at (800) 221-7945 ext. 5442 or by email at MacmillanSpecialMarkets@macmillan.com.

DISCLAIMER
The publisher and authors disclaim responsibility for any loss, injury, or damages that may result from a reader engaging in the activities described in this book.

TinkerActive is a trademark of Odd Dot.
Printed in China by Hung Hing Off-set Printing Co. Ltd., Heshan City, Guangdong Province
First edition, 2019

10 9 8 7 6 5 4 3 2 1

For the activity on page 73

For the activity on page 105

Sticker your **_TINKERACTIVE EXPERT_** poster after you complete each project.

For the activity on page 113

_____

(Your Name Here)

IS A TINKERACTIVE EXPERT!

PLACE YOUR MATH BADGE HERE!

PLACE YOUR SCIENCE BADGE HERE!

PLACE YOUR ENGLISH LANGUAGE ARTS BADGE HERE!

PROJECT 1　PROJECT 2　PROJECT 3
PROJECT 4　PROJECT 5　PROJECT 6
PROJECT 7　PROJECT 8　PROJECT 9
PROJECT 10　PROJECT 11　PROJECT 12
PROJECT 13　PROJECT 14　PROJECT 15

PROJECT 1　PROJECT 2　PROJECT 3
PROJECT 4　PROJECT 5　PROJECT 6
PROJECT 7　PROJECT 8　PROJECT 9
PROJECT 10　PROJECT 11　PROJECT 12
PROJECT 13　PROJECT 14　PROJECT 15

PROJECT 1　PROJECT 2　PROJECT 3
PROJECT 4　PROJECT 5　PROJECT 6
PROJECT 7　PROJECT 8　PROJECT 9
PROJECT 10　PROJECT 11　PROJECT 12
PROJECT 13　PROJECT 14　PROJECT 15

 COLLECT THEM ALL!